Teaching with Technology: Creating Student-Centered Classrooms

Teaching with Technology: Creating Student-Centered Classrooms

Judith Haymore Sandholtz
Cathy Ringstaff
David C. Dwyer

Foreword by Larry Cuban

Teachers College, Columbia University
New York and London

Published by Teachers College Press, 1234 Amsterdam Avenue, New York, N.Y. 10027

Portions of this book are adapted from articles that originally appeared in the journals *Educational Leadership, Journal of Educational Computing,* and *People and Education,* and from material in the book *Education and Technology: Reflections on Computing in Classrooms* (1996, Jossey-Bass). Used by permission of the copyright holders.

The research on which this book is based was supported by Apple Computer, Inc., the National Science Foundation under Grant No. TPE9253268, and the National Center for Education and the Economy. Any opinions, findings, conclusions, or recommendations expressed in this book are those of the authors and do not necessarily reflect the views of these organizations.

All photographs provided courtesy of Apple Computer, Inc.

Library of Congress Cataloging-in-Publication Data

Sandholtz, Judith.
    Teaching with technology : creating student-centered classrooms   /
  Judith Sandholtz, Cathy Ringstaff, David C. Dwyer ; foreword by
  Larry Cuban.
        p.   cm.
    Includes bibliographical references (p.   ) and index.
    ISBN 0–8077–3586–8 (paper : alk. paper). — ISBN 0–8077–3587–6
  (cloth : alk. paper)
    1. Apple Classrooms of Tomorrow (Project)   2. Computer-assisted
  instruction—United States—Case studies.   3. Educational
  technology—United States—Case studies.   4. Active learning—United
  States—Case studies.   5. Classroom management—United States—Case
  studies.   I. Ringstaff, Cathy.   II. Dwyer, David C.   III. Title.
  LB1028.5.S235   1996
  371.3'34—dc20   96–34755

ISBN 0-8077-3586-8 (paper)
ISBN 0-8077-3587-6 (cloth)

Printed on acid-free paper.
Manufactured in the United States of America

04   03   02   01   00   99   98   97   8   7   6   5   4   3   2   1

Contents

Foreword

The facts about the increasing use of information technologies in public schools are stunning. In the last decade alone, the number of students per computer went from 125 to less than 10. In some technology-rich schools, there is one computer for every three students.

Experts attribute this tremendous surge in acquisitions to sweeping changes in the workplace, where faxes, computer-linked networks, and e-mail have altered daily routines. Business officials, public policymakers, and parents—turning to low-tech schools—have pressed educators to get students ready to compete in a high-tech workplace. Besides giving the obvious economic reasons—that is, to keep pace with the demands of a swiftly changing economy—techno-enthusiasts have billed the new machines as energetic tools for making both learning and teaching for students and teachers more productive and engaging. For school boards and superintendents, these new machines, with far more interactive power than any of the earlier technologies such as film and television could ever muster in classrooms, have become a must.

Yet a peek behind the glitz of having computers in labs and classrooms reveals many tarnishes:

- Students' access to computers in American schools varies greatly by social class, race, and native language. Affluent, white, English-speaking students use computers more than their less affluent, nonwhite, nonnative-speaking peers.

- Low-achieving students are less likely to use machines to enhance reasoning and problem solving and more likely to use them for drill and practice.

- Uneven access means that individual students who use computers (and not all do) spend only one to two hours a week on the machine (or about 5% of all instructional time).

- What students do with computers varies greatly also. For example, high school students seldom use computers in academic subjects. Where they are used, the purpose has been to teach about computers.

■ Most teachers are casual users or nonusers; a small cadre of serious users have pioneered computer uses in their classrooms and schools.

How to account for this contradiction of remarkable gains in accessibility to computers and major inconsistencies in teacher and student use of these machines? Whenever classroom use of machines has failed to match the initial claims made on behalf of a new technology, techno-enthusiasts in this century have turned to the most obvious candidate for explaining why students don't use these wonder-machines: teachers. After all, in the age-graded school, where self-contained classrooms make teachers gatekeepers for what innovations enter, get adapted, or die, they become the obvious—if unwilling—target for blame. Reform-minded technophiles have historically been teacher-bashers. They have blamed nonusing teachers for being out of step with the introduction of film, radio, and television to classrooms before and since World War II. Ditto for computers.

Techno-enthusiasts then and now have framed the problem of limited and unimaginative use of information technologies as one of teachers lacking access to up-to-date hardware and software, being inadequately prepared to use the machines, and being without sufficient help to maintain and use them properly. With the problem defined in this narrow way, the solutions to limited use of technologies would seem to be more machines, accessible technical assistance, and better preparation in professional programs. Yet in framing the problem in this way, technology-minded reformers have ignored obvious questions.

Suppose that the problem were reframed from the point of view of a teacher. Given that I am expected to maintain order and get students to learn essential skills, knowledge, and values, how will these machines help or hinder my mission? Redefined in this way, very different questions emerge: What do teachers believe about learning and teaching that is relevant to these new technologies? How do these beliefs govern daily teaching practices? What criteria do teachers use in judging where, when, and under what conditions they will use a new machine? These are basic questions that begin from a base of respect for the impossible tasks that face teachers when they enter classrooms each day.

This book's authors, once teachers themselves, have asked these and other questions in offering readers the results of 10 years of working closely with scores of teachers in initially five Apple Classrooms of Tomorrow (ACOT) sites across the country, including three sites that have served as teacher development centers since 1992. They are the right questions to ask.

The Apple researchers who framed the original inquiry into class-rooms, in which computers were given to each teacher and student (in school and for the family), were wise enough to let the investigation evolve as teachers slowly changed their beliefs and classroom practices. They let teachers speak of their initial fears and turmoil in using computers and tell how the journey from being a nonuser to a serious one involved making major changes in daily routines. The lessons the authors assemble for readers are straightforward, not exotic; they are mundane, not thrilling. And, I must add, they are powerful in their implications.

From five classrooms located in five different schools in which children, families, and teachers received computers and accessories, ACOT researchers learned soon enough that a saturation strategy failed to alter how teachers taught (and, worse, excited envy else-where in the school). The researchers watched what happened, listened to teachers, and documented small, incremental, but significant changes in classroom practices. They recorded how classrooms became places of traditional and nontraditional teaching, imaginative hybrids of practice that emerged over time. They saw that turning these settings into centers so that teachers themselves could train peers accelerated and strengthened the learning (without necessarily reducing the inevitable frustrations accompanying these changes).

These researchers believe that a threshold level of classroom technology—far less than a computer for each child—can slowly, over time, transform traditional classrooms into student-centered places. They not only believe this, but they offer readers evidence of once-traditional teachers becoming coaches, helping students use software imaginatively to integrate it into the existing curriculum, while changing it far beyond where they began.

As a long-time skeptic of techno-enthusiast claims about new machines, I found their argument and evidence drawn from a decade's work in classrooms and teacher development sites (1992–1995) most persuasive. The nontraditional classroom practices that they sought did indeed materialize, albeit with much support from Apple. Computers were tools drafted to help create student-centered class-rooms. The overall goal was to create different forms of learning and teaching with the help of technology, not have technology determine what was to be learned or how it was to be taught. In making this crucial point Judith Sandholtz, Cathy Ringstaff, and David Dwyer have made a fine contribution to the continuing debate over school reform and the role that technology plays in helping teachers use machines both appropriately and imaginatively.

No reform-minded technophile, after reading this book, can ignore these important findings from the decadelong ACOT experience. As this study shows, it would be short-sighted, if not altogether misbegotten, to blame teachers for not being serious or imaginative users of new machines and software without considering the context for teaching, teacher beliefs about learning and teaching (and how hard it is a journey to alter those beliefs), and the crucial importance of school-site professional development.

No skeptic, after reading this book, can ignore the solid evidence that the authors provide of deep, lasting changes in teaching practices—the Holy Grail sought by reformers—that occurred over time in the classrooms they describe.

Few books can engage both doubters and true believers simultaneously. This is one of the few that will. Yet the policy implications of this study point powerfully toward those suggestions made by careful practitioners and researchers: Know where you want to go, and figure out how information technologies will help you get there; determine the optimal classroom-and-school mix of hardware and software; involve teachers deeply and continuously in their on-site learning, and then hang in with them as the inevitable squalls of turmoil blow and recede; and finally, have patience, for such changes in belief and practice will take years.

Larry Cuban

Preface

If you spend any time at all watching good teachers at work, it does not take long to understand that you are witnessing an artful and many-faceted juggling act. Defying gravity, teachers alternately spin, balance, and toss knowledge of where students are and where they need to go; insights into students' special needs and progress; choices of curricular activities and materials; rules that govern children's participation; expectations from parents and communities; and, of course, the norms and rules that govern them as teachers. At the side of the stage are judges, evaluating their performances and recommending changes as their acts unfold. Now, how about tossing in just one more ball—technology? What happens?

The question is as relevant now as it was in 1985 when teachers from five elementary and secondary schools around the United States volunteered to begin work with a project seeking an answer to that question. At the time pundits promised a virtual reformation of schooling with the advent of educational technology. Others decried the very thought of the unrelenting logic of computers guiding the minds and habits of children. The simple fact was that no one knew what the result of teachers and children routinely using technology for learning would be.

The project, Apple Classrooms of Tomorrow (ACOT), is a research collaboration between universities, public schools, and Apple Computer, Inc. Over the years, particularly in the area of teacher staff development, the project also gained sponsorship from the National Science Foundation and the New America Schools Development Corporation in conjunction with the National Alliance for Restructuring Education. This book is dedicated to the project's teachers and to telling their story. Our hope is that their experience and our analysis might help teachers, administrators, parents, and policymakers reconsider their expectations about technology use in schools. Our perspective is based on 10 years of systematic gathering of data, including teachers' personal accounts of their experiences in ACOT classrooms. All former classroom teachers, we held different roles within the ACOT project. Judith Sandholtz and Cathy Ringstaff served as outside researchers for the project, specifically focusing on teachers' experiences. David Dwyer both directed and studied the project in his position as Project Manager.

The story begins with an overview of the project and its history, which proved to be remarkably dynamic, changing as rapidly as the technologies and as definitively as the teachers themselves. Chapter 1 sets the foundation for how classroom instruction shifted from a reliance on lecture/recitation and drill and practice to a balanced approach that also included knowledge-construction activities.

Chapter 2 introduces Elizabeth Bennett and Christine Lee and traces their frustrations and worries, their plans and successes as they accommodated technology in their classrooms. We witness the potential of technology as a catalyst for change in both of their stories but also encounter the powerful forces which slow or prevent fundamental change in teachers' practices. Both teachers' stories highlight the personal commitment and energy that innovative projects like this one require.

Chapter 3 presents a five-stage model of the evolution of teacher practice and ties that evolution to the beliefs teachers hold about learning and about their roles as teachers—beliefs that accrue from their own experiences as students, from their training, and from the contexts in which they work. The introduction of technology as a routine tool for learning prompted catalytic, driving changes in the kinds of work that teachers and students engaged in, the manner in which they interacted, and the kinds of learning products that students created and demonstrated. This chapter concludes with suggestions for supporting teachers through the evolution, perhaps minimizing some of the anxiety and wasted effort that teachers may experience on their own.

Chapters 4 through 7 examine how the introduction of technology changed the dynamics of the ACOT classrooms. Chapter 4 begins, "If I had my druthers, I don't think I would ever look at a computer again." These words, spoken by one of the project's high school teachers, accurately reflect the down side of the love-hate relationship many of the teachers understandably had in ACOT's first year. In many ways, the massive introduction of technology forced teachers back into a first-year-teacher mode, starting all over again with issues of classroom management, discipline, role definition, and lesson development. None, in the early days, had any idea how they would come to depend on technology for teaching and how profoundly it would affect the way they taught. The up side, as teachers gained confidence and experience, included enhanced efficiency in record management, rapid student feedback, individualized instruction, more engaged students, and fewer discipline problems—even improved communication with parents.

Sage on the stage or guide on the side? Chapter 5 details the story of how technology proved to be a catalyst that helped teachers in the project make the transition to more facilitative roles. The shift is not an easy one. It challenges teachers' beliefs about their identity as teachers, their authority base, and their notion about the value they bring to teaching. But in their technology-rich classrooms, ACOT teachers confronted new realities, including the simple fact that children learn about and master technology far more rapidly than adults. This simple fact proved to be a powerful point of leverage that disturbed traditional classroom operation and led to real classroom innovation.

Chapter 6 may well address a new problem in the annals of school experience. What happens when students will not stop working? This unfamiliar territory proved encouraging to ACOT teachers, since it provided evidence that their hard work and perseverance with the technology had direct and dramatic payoffs. Students worked harder when they used technology. As one teacher put it: "They actually ask for things to do. In all of my years of teaching, I never had anyone ask for another ditto." Students' motivation stirred others. ACOT classrooms became busy places where clocks and bells were interruptions to students' self-directed activities—even when the bells signaled recess or lunch. Student work extended into the home, and traditional boundaries between school and home activities broke down. But like other aspects of the ACOT story, there were down sides. Engaged students dug deeply into their projects, threatening "coverage" of the curricular scope and sequence. Time management became a bigger issue for teachers. They were constantly challenged to stay ahead of their students, to provide new projects, and to find ways to evaluate what had been accomplished. The teachers also found that even ACOT students reached saturation points and would declare, Enough technology, already! This aspect of the ACOT experience helped us understand the limitations of the research on "time on task" in classrooms, which is often measured in short snippets of the instructional year. By focusing on longer learning episodes, we could understand conditions necessary to sustain student engagement over longer periods of time.

Early in ACOT's history, visitors and project researchers noted the surprising amount of interactions between the teachers. In some instances they shared large, double rooms and came to work together routinely. Or they visited back and forth between their own rooms, helping students as they passed through, providing technical assistance on demand. As the teams solidified over the years, team teaching became a hallmark of many ACOT learning environments. Chapter 7 focuses on this feature and makes the case that teacher collaboration is vital in the implementation of complex innovations in classrooms. However, the development of stable teacher teams is difficult, hampered by strong personalities and the desire for autonomy but driven by the need to help one another in the fast moving, challenging world of technology-rich classrooms.

Chapter 8 describes a support process called the unit of practice, which ACOT created to help teachers integrate technology into the curriculum. The chapter relates the experience of Dan Tate as he integrated technology into one of his most successful teaching episodes, "Journey Through the Twentieth Century." Through the process, Mr. Tate changed not only components of the unit itself but also his views about teaching and learning.

Later cadres of ACOT teachers moved through the stages of instructional evolution described in Chapter 3 faster than did the initial project participants. The explanation for this acceleration was evident in teacher interviews. Newcomers became constructively immersed in situations where they could observe and work with the seasoned ACOT teachers and their students, who demonstrated daily the kinds of work that could be accomplished with technology. In addition, new teachers found themselves surrounded by sources of technical help, inspiration, and proof of what can happen with meaningful use of technology. In 1991 a steering committee composed of ACOT teachers and staff considered the implications of their experience for teacher staff development related to technology and learning. Were there a few general principles that could be derived and applied in a formal teacher professional development program? This question led to funding from the National Science Foundation, a new mission for three of ACOT's oldest sites, and a powerful professional experience for hundreds of teachers from schools and districts throughout the country. Chapters 9 and 10 chronicle teachers' experiences at ACOT's teacher development centers and describe productive elements of environments that encourage teacher learning and promote change in teacher practices. Chapter 9 describes teachers' experiences at the teacher development centers, and Chapter 10 documents what happened when participants returned to their own schools.

Technology has potential to change education in beneficial ways, but only under certain circumstances. In the concluding chapter, we examine key conditions that we believe are necessary for technology to have a productive influence on teaching and learning. We conclude the book as we began it—with the voices of teachers. Without their willingness to share their experiences, this research could not have been undertaken. We gratefully acknowledge the ACOT teachers and coordinators and their pioneering efforts, dedication, and hard work. Even with the additional pressures that technology added to their already full workloads, they managed to share their concerns and triumphs, which enabled us to provide a rich description of life in technology-rich classrooms. Participants in the Teacher Development Center project also gave willingly of their time. Their experiences gave us further insight into the constraints teachers face and the supports they need as they integrate technology into their classrooms.

We also acknowledge the contributions of ACOT staff, past and present, with special thanks to Keith Yocam, Jacqui Celsi, Connie Troy-Downing, and Cynthia Bautista for their encouragement throughout the process of completing this book. We appreciate the assistance of the following individuals: Lorraine Aochi, Lynda Stone, Barbara Stumpp, and Jeanne Woodward. Our editor at Teachers College Press, Faye Zucker, enthusiastically supported our work, provided helpful feedback, and encouraged us when deadlines loomed large.

Similar to the advantages of teacher and student collaboration that we describe in this book, we profited from collaborating as co-authors. This work was a team effort facilitated by the use of technology. As we used technology to study technology, we increasingly identified with many of the frustrations and benefits the ACOT teachers encountered in their classrooms.

Finally, we appreciate the ongoing support of our immediate and extended families. They continue to encourage us and find ways for us to pursue our professional endeavors. Special thanks to Wayne Sandholtz, whose devotion to family benefited us all, and to Baby Will, whose playful antics and toothless smiles humored us and kept the project in perspective. Our daughters, Sarah and Stephanie, reinforced our observations about children's inquisitive nature and their need for an active learning environment. Through the conception and completion of this book, our children were pleasant and constant reminders about what is most important in our lives.

Judith Haymore Sandholtz
Cathy Ringstaff
David C. Dwyer

This book draws upon previously published work by the authors:

Dwyer, D. C. (1994). Apple Classrooms of Tomorrow: What we've learned. *Educational Leadership, 51*(7), 4–10.

Dwyer, D. C. (1996). The imperative to change our schools. In C. Fisher, D. C. Dwyer, & K. Yocam (Eds.), *Education and technology: Reflections on computing in classrooms* (pp. 15–33). San Francisco: Jossey-Bass.

Dwyer, D. C., Ringstaff, C., & Sandholtz, J. H. (1991). Changes in teachers' beliefs and practices in technology-rich classrooms. *Educational Leadership, 48*(8), 45–52.

Ringstaff, C., Sandholtz, J. H., & Dwyer, D. C. (1994). Trading places: When teachers use student expertise in technology-intensive classrooms. *People and Education, 2*(4) , 405–430.

Sandholtz, J. H., Ringstaff, C., & Dwyer, D. C. (1992). Teaching in high-tech environments: Classroom management revisited. *Journal of Educational Computing, 8*(4), 479–505.

Sandholtz, J. H., Ringstaff, C., & Dwyer, D. C. (1995). The relationship between technological innovation and collegial interaction. *People and Education, 3*(3), 295–321.

Teaching with Technology: Creating Student-Centered Classrooms

1

From Instruction
to Construction

66 Sam (a primary-grade student): *"I don't know if we'll have computers [next year].
If we don't, it will be weird. 'Cause the teacher talks pretty long and you have to listen."*

Sam's mother: *"He's really into it—I think computers are just part of our lives now.
And it hasn't made Sam any less in terms of wanting to read, or paint or draw. And
he's really proud."*

Sam's teacher: *"I think [computers are] going to help me. It's not going to hurt
[students]. I think that they are going to get as much out of working on the computers
as they will out of working out of workbooks. I think. But see, I'm not even 100%
sure on that."* **99**

1

A primary-grade teacher, Lynn Broderick,[1] has taken the first steps toward integrating technology into her classroom. Her student reports his ready acceptance of computers and, with the guilelessness of the very young, contrasts his experience with an imagined return to a computerless room where "the teacher talks pretty long and you have to listen" (Phelan, 1989). The child's mother also expresses her satisfaction with the computer-intensive program. But Ms. Broderick, a volunteer in the Apple Classrooms of Tomorrow (ACOT) project, is ambivalent. Will her students do as well with the technology as with her traditional use of workbooks? She's not sure. Like most teachers, she has seen educational fads come and go. She wonders if the classroom use of computers and other technology will disappear like other innovations designed to revolutionize education.

Ms. Broderick's concerns about technology are understandable. Educational reforms frequently fail: "There should be a page in the *Guinness Book of Records* on failed classroom reforms, for few ever seem to have been incorporated into teachers' repertoires" (Cuban, 1984, p. 6). However, computers and other types of technology are becoming increasingly pervasive, even in school settings. Over a 10-year period, the percentage of U.S. schools with at least one computer for instructional use increased from 18% to 98%; over roughly the same period, the number of students per computer shifted from 125 to 18 (Means, 1994).

Now that technology is becoming more common in schools, its potential for enhancing teaching and learning is being recognized. Technologies are described as essential tools of the teaching trade, yet research has focused almost exclusively on the impact of technology on students with little investigation of the implications for teachers (Office of Technology Assessment, 1995). This failure to explore teachers' experiences with technology must be remedied. Teachers need to be at the center of reform efforts, both as active participants and as leaders in change. Educational reform depends on what teachers think and do (Fullan & Stiegelbauer, 1991). Ultimately, they determine what happens in the classroom and how innovations are, or are not, implemented. Teachers need to know that they play a role in changing their work environment and that this change can make a difference (Kelley, 1994). Like Cuban (1986), we believe that teachers are the gateway to change and that ultimately they will determine whether technology will significantly influence education.

Teachers naturally wonder if the benefits of using technology outweigh the extra effort required of them to integrate technology

---

1. Pseudonyms are used throughout the book.

into their instruction. Changing the classroom environment to include technology may not eliminate many of the age-old problems inherent in the school system and, in some cases, may exacerbate them. Limited time, pressure to cover the mandated curriculum, problems with classroom management, scarce resources, and teachers' feelings of isolation persist even in classrooms radically altered by the introduction of new technological tools. This book addresses teachers' concerns in today's settings, drawing directly from their experiences over 10 years in the Apple Classrooms of Tomorrow project. Looking at their experiences over time provides an opportunity to examine not only challenges but also solutions and benefits of working in technology-rich classrooms. This book gives teachers who are learning to use technology a road map for their journey. By knowing what to expect, they may realize that the potholes and bumps they come across along the way are a natural part of the experience. Once they get past these obstacles, we believe the benefits make the journey worth the effort.

THE APPLE CLASSROOMS OF TOMORROW (ACOT) PROJECT

ACOT, a research-and-development collaboration among public schools, universities, research agencies, and Apple Computer began in 1985, a time when promises and excitement about the potential of technology to enhance the learning process abounded. Visionaries promised that technology would someday be as common as paper and pencils, and would revitalize America's ailing educational system: "We are at a point in the history of education when radical change is possible, and the possibility for that change is directly tied to the impact of the computer" (Papert, 1980, pp. 36–37). This optimism, however, rested on thin evidence, since scant research had yet been conducted examining the effects of computers on education.

The ACOT project set out to investigate how routine use of technology by teachers and students would affect teaching and learning. At the beginning of the project, the stated goals were to work collaboratively with educators to

- install and operate computer-saturated classrooms as living laboratories in every grade (K–12)
- integrate state-of-the-art technologies into the instructional fabric of schooling
- bring about positive educational development and change

■ study and understand the impact of total computer access on students, teachers, and instructional processes

ACOT worked from within Apple Computer's research think tank, independent of the company's product, sales, and marketing divisions.

After soliciting and reviewing proposals from interested school districts, ACOT began work in five schools in four states. The initial sites represented a cross section of America's K–12 schools in terms of grade level, socioeconomic status, and community setting. Each of these five ACOT sites began with one classroom, then added classrooms, staff, and students in subsequent years. Although each site served students from a variety of grade levels, none of the sites encompassed an entire school.[2] ACOT staff asked that the gender and ethnic composition of the classes mirror the school as a whole; all other decisions about student selection were left up to school personnel. In addition, the sites developed key objectives on which to concentrate during their first year with the project. Table 1.1 summarizes the characteristics and objectives of the original sites.

ACOT equipped project classrooms with computers, printers, scanners, laser-disc and videotape players, modems, CD-ROM drives, and a variety of software packages. ACOT provided each participating teacher and student two computers, one for the home and one for the classroom. Since hardware in 1986 was big and heavy, the two-computer formula was the only way to simulate a time when students and teachers would have constant access to technology by virtue of some future state of miniaturization, portability, and cost.

Project teachers were all volunteers selected by the individual school districts. The teachers ranged from novices with 1 or 2 years of experience to veterans with over 20 years in the classroom. Few had worked closely with technology before joining the project. They ranged in age from their mid-twenties to mid-fifties and represented various ethnic backgrounds. At the elementary sites most of the project teachers were female, but at the high school site the number of male and female project teachers was about the same. ACOT staff provided training for teachers on telecommunications, basic troubleshooting, and tool software such as spreadsheets, databases, and graphics programs. ACOT also helped fund a coordinator at each site to provide technical and instructional assistance.

---

2. In 1995, ACOT moved to a new elementary site and now involves an entire school.

Table 1.1 Summary of ACOT site characteristics—year 1

Site Location	Northern Great Plains	West Coast	Great Lakes	South (School A)	South (School B)
School enrollment	1,000	348	1,300	1,132	750
Grade levels	K–12	K–6	9–12	K–6	K–6
Community	Rural	Suburban	Urban	Suburban	Inner city
Socio-economic status	Middle	Middle and upper-middle	Lower-middle	Lower-middle and middle	Lower
Student ethnicity	99% Caucasian 1% other	85% Caucasian 15% other	50% Caucasian 50% other	70% Caucasian 30% other	100% African-American
ACOT grade level	5th	3rd	9th	4th	5th
Number of ACOT students	25	30	30	24	30
Number of computers					
Apple IIe	31	34	5	33	32
Apple IIc	31	34	0	29	40
Macintosh	1	2	70	3	3
Key objectives	Individualize math and reading	Integrate computers into primary grade curriculum and instruction	Integrate generic software into high school curriculum	Integrate computers into 4th grade instruction	Support student homework through modem tutoring
	Network with Apple IIe's	Teach higher order thinking skills	Network Macintosh computers		

ACOT's early vision about the role of technology in education went far beyond the simplistic notion of computers as teaching machines. Technology was viewed as a tool to support learning across the curriculum. Therefore no attempt was made to replace existing instructional technologies with computers. Instead, project classrooms included—along with computers—multiple instructional resources such as textbooks, workbooks, manipulative math materials, crayons, and pianos. The operating principle in ACOT classrooms was to use the tool that best supported the learning goal.

Over the years, the number of students, teachers, classrooms and sites involved with the project changed. For example, in 1989 ACOT staff reduced the project's focus to three sites so that they could work intensively with fewer schools. Classrooms at these three sites continued to be added so that students could be followed through more grades.

Other changes at ACOT sites related to the amount, type, and configuration of technology. Small classrooms, large numbers of students, and heavy computers often presented a serious barrier to technology use. We learned that computer access was important but that access did not necessarily require a computer on every desk. Although there were times when every student needed his or her own computer, a smaller number of computers in the classroom would have sufficed. Smaller and lighter computers have made it easier for teachers and students to share equipment. Consequently, rather than providing each student with home and school computers, the configuration of ACOT classrooms shifted in later years to require the sharing of resources. Also, ACOT continued providing home computers at only one high school site. ACOT stopped supplying home computers to elementary students because their teachers did not have time to develop appropriate assignments.

The use of technology in ACOT classrooms also changed over the years because the technology itself changed. New types of software programs emerged, leading to new opportunities. For example, students learned to create multimedia projects that were unheard of 10 years earlier. Advances in telecommunications allowed students access to a vast amount of information. Hardware improvements in memory capacity, speed, and networking capability had important implications for what teachers and students could accomplish. These technological advances became catalysts for change because they raised new instructional issues.

ACOT'S RESEARCH PROGRAM

Although ACOT staff provided training and support for teachers in response to their expressed needs, the early stages of the project operated in the mode of a laissez-faire experiment. ACOT staff did not try to hold variables constant to test theories. Instead, they supported a generative model, encouraging variation and change. Rather than imposing an agenda, the staff let events unfold and evolve. The initial guiding question of the research was simply put: What happens when teachers and students have constant access to technology? No attempts were made at this point to promote pedagogical change as teachers and students adjusted to these high-technology classrooms.

To investigate the impact of technology on project classrooms, ACOT sponsored research involving more than 20 universities and research institutions. For example, some researchers examined student writing, students' thought processes, and student empowerment in ACOT settings. Others developed technological learning tools to enhance understanding of subject areas such as physics and calculus.

The research on which this book is based focused specifically on teachers' experiences in these technology-rich classrooms. Teachers provided certain data to ACOT staff on an ongoing basis. The project asked each teacher to reflect into an audiotape recorder every few weeks. In these audiotape journals, teachers recorded their personal observations of events in their classrooms and their reflections on those events. Rather than asking teachers to comment on any particular aspect of their teaching, instructions about content on the tapes were purposefully left vague, giving teachers the freedom to report what was most salient to each of them at the time. They often used the tapes to vent their frustrations and share their triumphs, giving the tapes an emotionally charged quality.

In addition to audiotapes, each site generated a weekly report that communicated major events. These were electronically distributed among all project participants, including administrative staff and teaching colleagues. Project teachers also corresponded with each other over an electronic networking system. Teachers initiated this communication and typically solicited or offered information related to software programs, equipment, or classroom activities. In contrast to the audiotapes, the written entries were much less personal and introspective. The audiotape journals, weekly reports, and site correspondence gave us an ongoing pipeline into the ACOT classrooms and allowed us to capture and describe the complexity of what was happening in the lives of these teachers and students. We created two databases, using the actual text information generated in the audiotapes, weekly reports, and site correspondence. These databases, which contained over 20,000 entries, allowed us to systematically query the equivalent of 5,000 single-spaced pages of prose (see the appendix for information on data collection and analysis).

In 1992 our research took on a new direction when ACOT received a grant from the National Science Foundation (NSF) to create a replicable model of staff development designed to help teachers from throughout the country integrate technology into their classrooms and learn about constructivist teaching approaches. Drawing on years of experience in the school sites, a steering committee composed of ACOT staff, teachers, administrators, and researchers structured the model around a set of guiding principles about learning, technology, and staff development. These principles, which are discussed in Chapter 9, provide a framework that can guide other schools and districts as they create staff development programs.

ACOT established teacher development centers at three of ACOT's oldest sites.[3] Over a three-year period, over 600 teachers representing 15 states and two foreign countries attended one-week practicums or four-week summer institutes. At this stage of ACOT's evolution, our research shifted to examining the effectiveness of this model of staff development. We expanded our data collection strategies to include interviews, questionnaires, and extensive observations at each site. In addition, selected participants and their schools became the focus of in-depth case studies.

WHAT WE LEARNED: A HISTORICAL OVERVIEW

In the beginning of the project, we thought that technology would be used to support individualized learning, self-expression through writing, and drill and practice. Aside from more freedom for students to work at their own pace, we expected a smooth integration of technology into fairly traditional classrooms. We anticipated that students

---

3. Seven additional staff development sites were created through a partnership with the National Alliance for Restructuring Education in 1992. These centers were based on the NSF-supported teacher development model. Research discussed in this book draws primarily on data collected at the original ACOT sites and three NSF-funded teacher development centers.

could learn more efficiently with the simple addition of this new instructional tool.

During the first few years, the addition of technology did not revolutionize classroom instruction. Although the sheer number of computers and other technologies in ACOT classrooms radically transformed the physical environment, for the most part student learning tasks remained unchanged. Teachers successfully translated a text-dominated, lecture–recitation–seat work instructional approach to an electronic medium. To compensate for the amount of time and effort they were putting into developing new technology skills and new classroom management strategies, even teachers who had previously favored small-group, multitask instruction temporarily resorted to whole-group, direct instruction.

While the addition of technology failed to substantially change students' learning tasks in this phase of the project, our research began to identify other kinds of changes. We saw teachers begin to question long-held beliefs about the purpose and nature of instruction (Chapters 2 and 3). We documented teachers' struggles and triumphs as they created new strategies for managing their high-technology classrooms (Chapter 4). We noticed that teachers began to interact differently with students—more as guides or mentors and less as lecturers—and that cooperative and task-related interaction among ACOT students was spontaneous and more extensive than in traditional classrooms (Chapter 5). Student interest in and engagement with technology did not decline with routine use, despite some teachers' fears that the novelty of computer use would wear off and students would become bored (Chapter 6). And, collegial sharing among project teachers began to increase as they sought support from one another (Chapter 7).

As the project progressed, changes in classrooms became striking. Teachers began teaming and working across the disciplines. Administrators and teachers modified school schedules to accommodate unusually ambitious class projects. In addition, teachers and students began demonstrating mastery of technology, frequently integrating several kinds of media in their lessons or projects. ACOT classrooms became an interesting mix of the traditional and nontraditional. Teachers experimented with new types of tasks for students. In addition to becoming comfortable with new patterns of collegial interaction, they also encouraged far more collaboration among their students. In most instances, teachers altered the physical setup of their classrooms and modified daily schedules to permit students more time to work on projects. They also provided more opportunities for students to use a broader mix of learning and communication tools. Finally, teachers struggled with the need for new methods of evaluation that could capture the novel ways that students were demonstrating their mastery of skills and concepts. At most sites experimentation with performance- and portfolio-based assessment began.

Other research investigating the impact of technology on education supports ACOT's findings. For example, a study on the potential of interactive learning tools for improving the quality of education reported that one of the most significant outcomes of the use of computers in the classroom has been a change in teachers' roles from the "traditional presenters of ready-made knowledge" to facilitators of student learning (Office of Technology Assessment, 1988). Similarly, in an examination of 133 research reviews and reports on educational technology, researchers concluded that technology encouraged student-centered, cooperative learning but that the impact of technology on the learning environment evolves over an extended period of time (Mehlinger, 1996). Moreover, technology implementation often inspires teachers to use more complex tasks and materials in their instruction (Means, 1994).

ACOT'S CHANGING MISSION

As we witnessed the gradual changes in ACOT classrooms, we came to view technology in classrooms very differently. We learned that meaningful use of technology in schools goes far beyond just dropping it into schools. Technology in and of itself will not change education; what matters is how it is used. At this point, ACOT staff actively encouraged and supported teachers' efforts to create environments where technologies were used as knowledge-building tools for communication and collaboration, media-rich composition, and simulation and modeling across the curriculum. ACOT staff wanted project classrooms to become places where students were more active, where interaction among them was ordinary and purposeful, and where children were not always novices but sometimes experts. They wanted students to routinely work on problems with no simple answers and to look at math, science, language arts, and social studies not as distinct subject areas but as different lenses to broaden perspective and deepen understanding. In short, ACOT's vision for education began to contrast sharply with traditional approaches to teaching, such as those described in the next section.

REAL SCHOOL

If you close your eyes and imagine a classroom, chances are great that you will picture an adult standing at the front of a room that contains 30 or so students sitting in straight rows of desks. Students are likely to be doing one of three things: listening to the teacher lecture, raising their hands to participate in a whole class recitation, or working quietly and independently on some written exercise. Closely allied with this scene are assumptions about the organizational basics of schools: textbooks and courses of study set by the central office, mandatory attendance, grade levels, and testing. Metz (1988) calls this common image "real school." It is so pervasive that other forms of schooling for young Americans seem unimaginable (Sizer, 1984). Real school exists not only in our minds but is, in fact, what most of our children encounter five days a week in their schools.

During the 1980s, schools engaging in these traditional forms of instruction seemed remarkably successful at increasing student test scores in basic skills such as reading and math, a trend reflected in reports of the Iowa Tests of Basic Skills, the Stanford Achievement Test, and the National Assessment of Educational Progress (Bracey, 1991; Cuban, 1991). On the other hand, Applebee, Langer, and Mullis (1989) reported that

> Sixty-one percent of the 17-year-old students could not read or understand relatively complicated material, such as that typically presented at the high school level. Nearly one-half appear to have limited mathematics skills and abilities that go little beyond adding, subtracting, and multiplying with whole numbers. More than one-half could not evaluate the procedures or results of a scientific study, and few included enough information in their written pieces to communicate their ideas effectively. Additionally, assessment results in other curriculum areas indicate that high school juniors have little sense of historical chronology, have not read much literature, tend to be unfamiliar with the uses and potential application of computers. (p. 26)

What was creating these disparate images of our educational well-being? How could student test scores be on the rise while student performance on complex tasks showed such abysmal results? One explanation discloses a bitter irony. When teachers and administrators became more accountable for student test scores, they increasingly limited instruction to drill and practice of the kinds of skills and disjointed facts that nationally normed tests emphasized. As a result of state-mandated accountability systems that began as early as 1972, "public schools showed a decline in the use of such methods as student-centered discussion, the writing of essays or themes, and projects or laboratory work" (Darling-Hammond, 1990, p. 290). In other words, while schools focused, albeit successfully, on raising test scores, the classroom demand for higher-order cognitive performance virtually disappeared. Students became better test takers, but at a terrible cost.

In response to this phenomenon, reform efforts around the country began to call for a move toward teaching practices that would emphasize problem solving, concept development, and critical thinking rather than rote memorization of facts (Carnegie Forum on Education and the Economy, 1986; Holmes Group, 1990). Such a reemphasis would require a dramatic shift in the form of instruction routine in American classrooms. ACOT began to view technology as a necessary and catalytic part of this shift.

SHIFTING FROM INSTRUCTION TO CONSTRUCTION

Adopting recommendations by groups such as the National Council for Teachers of Mathematics and the National Science Teachers Association, many teachers began to implement new instructional strategies based on a theory of knowledge and learning called constructivism. Constructivism is a theory that

> defines knowledge as temporary, developmental, socially and culturally mediated, and thus, non-objective. Learning from this perspective is understood as a self-regulating process of resolving inner cognitive conflicts that often become apparent through concrete experience, collaborative discourse, and reflection. (Brooks & Brooks, 1993, p. vii)

Teachers using a constructivist approach realize that learning is not only a matter of transferring ideas from one who is knowledgeable to one who is not—a view in which a teacher's work is construed as instruction. Instead, learning is perceived as a personal, reflective, and transformative process where ideas, experiences, and points of view are integrated and something new is created—a view where teacher work is construed as facilitating individuals' abilities to construct knowledge (Collins, 1991; Dwyer, 1994; Holmes Group, 1990; Sheingold, 1991). When applied in the context of schooling, this shift demands changes in deeply held beliefs about the form of classroom activities, the respective roles of teachers and students, the goals of instruction, the very concept of knowledge, and the definition and measurement of student success.

In an instruction classroom, activity is more often than not the domain of teachers. They are the ones with freedom to move about, to initiate actions and interactions, to allocate time and resources, to ask questions. They are the tellers of facts, the definers of important ideas. Students are, in the main, passive listeners and carefully choreographed followers. Conversely, in the knowledge construction classroom, this activity and freedom are at least shared with students. Action becomes the domain of learners, whether teachers or students. Usually teachers are experts, but other sources of expertise are recognized, valued, and used—even when the source of expertise is children, a common state of affairs in classrooms with technology.

In knowledge construction classrooms, teacher-student interactions are less didactic, more collaborative. Students work together. Learning environments feel more like real workplaces where problems are solved through conversation, inquiry, trial and error, and constant comparison of one approximate solution against another. Facts are important in these kinds of classrooms, but not solely for their own sake. The emphasis is on the processes of inquiry and invention that lead to the discovery of facts. Making sense from facts—discovering relationships or transformations from which students create a new order, a new pattern, a new understanding—is a paramount value.

The knowledge-building activities of students must not end with privately held constructions. Students' paraphrases, new ideas, models, drawings, and compositions need to be shared in a critical light. They need to be reviewed by peers, explained to parents, presented to expert panels, considered for entry into personal portfolios, and reviewed and assessed against rigorous standards. The process allows the discovery and correction of misconceptions while it gives purpose to learning tasks. Students need a sense that their work is important, that what they do matters, that other people will be interested in and care about what they discover. Sharing personal knowledge raises the stakes in classrooms. It introduces a sense of risk that makes students inquire more carefully and deeply.

The contrasting views of instruction and construction are summarized in Table 1.2. The cognitive premises of constructivism cannot dictate specific teaching methods but rather offer guidelines for good teaching (Noddings, 1990).

As different as knowledge instruction and knowledge construction are, they are not, as is often argued, incompatible. They can be

Table 1.2   Contrasting views of instruction and construction

	Instruction	Construction
Classroom activity	Teacher centered Didactic	Learner centered Interactive
Teacher role	Fact teller Always expert	Collaborator Sometimes learner
Student role	Listener Always learner	Collaborator Sometimes expert
Instructional emphasis	Facts Memorization	Relationships Inquiry and invention
Concept of knowledge	Accumulation of facts	Transformation of facts
Demonstration of success	Quantity	Quality of understanding
Assessment	Norm referenced Multiple-choice items	Criterion referenced Portfolios and performances
Technology use	Drill and practice	Communication, collaboration, information access, expression

viewed as different complementary positions on a continuum of possible learning strategies. Instruction—lecture, drill and practice—is an appropriate way to introduce skills or concepts, build awareness, or reinforce some set of actions that can be replayed habitually. For example, when students continue to make a certain kind of error in mathematics, it is reasonable to demonstrate how to do the procedure correctly and give them practice exercises (Noddings, 1990). Similarly, when breadth is valued over depth in curriculum, instruction is one way to make sure you cover the necessary content in a given amount of time.

When depth and understanding are the most desirable outcomes, however, knowledge construction is a better strategy to help learners personalize and deeply internalize ideas, to create situations where skills and concepts can be applied in different contexts to solve problems, to explore or generate ideas, and to generalize and synthesize knowledge. Teachers must reflect on their goals for children and select learning strategies that best accomplish those goals. The best prepared teachers are ones who can put a wide range of strategies to work for the benefit of their students.

While combining instruction and construction may seem a matter of common sense, it is not often done. The two approaches often raise serious debate, waged on philosophical, political, and even moral grounds (Cuban, 1990). The set of beliefs around instruction builds up in us all through our own lives as students. As we prepare to become teachers, those beliefs are reinforced by the lecture-dominated pedagogy of universities. When we arrive at our first teaching assignment, those same beliefs are formally sanctioned by administrators through evaluation practices and informally in the faculty lounge by other teachers. This process explains the intransigence of traditional schooling. In the end, we most likely teach as we were taught (Lortie, 1975). Learning to teach using a constructivist approach often requires a paradigm shift. "Becoming such a teacher means much more than appending new practices to already full repertoires. For many, it requires the willing abandonment of familiar perspectives and practices and the adoption of new ones" (Brooks & Brooks, 1993, p. 25). When technology is added to this challenge, the picture becomes even more complicated. The next chapter describes the experiences of two ACOT teachers as they attempted this difficult journey.

2

The Challenge of Instructional Change: Two Teachers' Stories

" *I guess I have to realize that what I am doing is learning how to undo my thinking.* **"**

This reflection by one of ACOT's teachers reinforces the fact that instructional change is not easy. The following two case studies describe the inner conflict involved in the process of instructional change. The more the classroom environment changed, the more teachers had to confront their beliefs about learning and the efficacy of their instructional activities. These episodic accounts of two teachers' experiences—based on their personal audiotape journals, weekly reports, and site correspondence—indicate that the process of integrating technology into classroom instruction was ridden with self-doubt, subject to external influence, exhausting, and never unidirectional.

Most teachers entering the ACOT project hoped that technology would make their jobs easier and more efficient. Most never dreamed they would alter their instructional approaches or broaden their perspectives about what children should and should not, could and could not, accomplish in their classrooms. Even though all of the teachers in the ACOT project had volunteered and were eager participants in an ambitious program whose espoused goal was change in instruction and learning, they were also experienced in traditional classrooms where they had spent years, first as students and later as teachers. They brought to the program, as part of their personal history, deeply held beliefs about schooling. The words of one teacher described the experience of many:

> As you work into using the computer in the classroom, you start
> questioning everything you have done in the past and wonder
> how you can adapt it to the computer. Then you start questioning
> the whole concept of what you originally did.

This kind of questioning led to experimentation. Successful experiments led to more experiments. Failures led to setbacks, even to temporary cessation of new strategies. But fundamental alterations in these classrooms—the intensity of student engagement, the extent of collaboration, the presence of the technology as a symbol of change—had their own momentum. Inexorably, teachers seemed drawn back to further exploration, while students collectively influenced events as they always do, expressing pleasure and displeasure clearly and persistently.

The direction of change was toward student-centered rather than curriculum-centered instruction, toward collaborative tasks rather than individual tasks, toward active rather than passive learning. Each of these dimensions brought deeply held beliefs about "real schools" into conflict with what teachers witnessed in their class-rooms. The conflict never transformed those beliefs outright. The process seemed more gradual: an erosion of the old, a building up of the new. During this process, teachers' actions would first swing one direction and then the other.

In the following case study, the teacher noticed increased student engagement when children had more choice and when lessons were less teacher directed. She was anxious, however, because student engagement was tightly coupled with computer use and student collaboration, which she associated with movement and noise. Movement and noise conflicted with her belief in classrooms as quiet and orderly places. The result is a story of vacillation.

ELIZABETH BENNETT: FIFTH GRADE

In ACOT's first year, Mrs. Bennett taught fifth grade in an inner-city school located in the middle of public housing projects. The school enrolled approximately 900 students, the majority of whom were classified as at risk. The school served as a demonstration site where educational innovations were developed and tested before being implemented elsewhere in the district. State mandates required teachers to concentrate heavily on basic skills in math and reading.

Establishing a Routine

In the first month of the ACOT project, Mrs. Bennett reflected on a lesson on cells and worried that her approach was too "teacher directed." Given her unfamiliarity with computers and software, however, she said that the students were going to have "to get used to following instructions." She established a familiar routine over the first three weeks of September, wherein she would present a lesson and then allow children to use their computers for individual practice and reinforcement drills. But she reported a small variation in the third week that resulted in increased student engagement.

> I struck on a new idea for the computers. Rather than use it as a follow up on text or teacher presentations, I have the children at their computers and have them turn off their monitors while I present, but I allow them to return to working on their own machines as the lesson progresses. I feel pretty good about using the software in this way. Attention is improved and every child is involved.

Experimenting

From this small success came several experiments. In the next several months, Mrs. Bennett established a free period, during which children could select any software with which to work. She began small-group instruction, which meant that children worked more on their own. Finally, she suggested a class newspaper project and allowed the students to choose editors and reporters and, in large part, run the activity.

But by early December she expressed a concern, one born from her knowledge that there was a set of curriculum objectives for which she was responsible.

> I would feel a lot more comfortable about some of the things that I do if I just knew that before the end of the year I really was going to be able to meet all the objectives and all the things that these children will need.

On the heels of this concern, students' free choice during free time ended abruptly:

> No more game-type programs in school as there is not enough time for this style of learning activity, which is noisy and creates too much excitement. It's become a problem instead of an asset, so I figured the best thing to do is get rid of the problem.

The newspaper project fared better because she saw very positive student outcomes—among them responsibility, skill development, and children helping one another, as this entry illustrates:

> Several children are writing more than one article. Considerable creativity and good self-expression are evident, but many errors will require careful proofreading. Students are correcting one another's work before publishing it on the computer.

By mid-December it was common to see children working together on projects in Mrs. Bennett's classroom. Children were more active and often performed several different curricular activities simultaneously. They also had more responsibility and exercised more choice. Reflecting on the status of her classroom, Mrs. Bennett noted:

> Old teaching friends were swapping "horror stories" about this year's problems, but the ACOT room has none to offer. A parent

also reported stories of problems in another school's fifth grade. Not everyone in the ACOT classroom is perfect, but I do not have the discipline problems that I have had in the past or that my friends are having this year. And I think the factor that I would say made the difference is the computers. Students are getting positive, immediate feedback; they're busy; the work is more appropriate because they have varied activities. I have more time to deal with problems.

This report is so glowing that one might assume smooth and continuous progress in Mrs. Bennett's effort to change instruction in her classroom. But immediately after the winter break, she made an abrupt about-face. In her tapes, she reported discipline problems and difficulties in controlling her class. She even questioned the benefit of students working together:

> Children don't pay attention. The nonlisteners can't pass a quiz on the vocabulary just discussed. Perhaps some students would stay on task better with a cubicle arrangement during individual work time.

The lapse was temporary. Less than a week later, Mrs. Bennett reported on a particularly satisfying science class involving the classification of birds, where children were again working together, actively involved in the lesson, and working at their own direction.

> I felt like there was real thinking going on. Once they completed one of the birds, they had no problem going on and doing the rest of them. This activity was a great help with classification skills. Children are very involved when they have to search for and enter information into their database. Every child in the class is involved.

She also noted that there was a price to pay for "involvement"—lots of students who wanted help at the same time. She wished that she were "about 10 different people at one time." With that comment, however, she also mentioned that "neighbors can help each other." But in action, this principle leads to noise and movement, and as the days passed, both became dominant themes in Mrs. Bennett's thoughts:

> Children are somewhat noisier as they become familiar with the equipment, and they talk a lot. Some of the moving-about routines could be smoothed out to keep a good learning

environment. There are many management changes with computers, disks, and new and unfamiliar responsibilities for both students and teacher.

Turning Back Toward Tradition

"Good learning environment" hearkens back to images of "real school," and in only a few days Mrs. Bennett again questioned her direction and made a turn toward tradition:

> Lots of noise results from the interaction of computer activities. Children talk and move around more than in conventional classrooms. Keeping noise and movement controlled is necessary.

She expressed concern about not having enough control in the classroom:

> The availability of software at individual workstations gives students too much control over what they elect to do. Some students choose to do things that are not relevant at the time. The software can be very tempting.

After making these comments, she returned to whole-group lecture and recitation activities. With satisfaction, she noted that her students were again quiet: "I see most improvement in the students' abilities to sit still, listen attentively, and enjoy stories."

"Real school" had returned with a vengeance: with it came a period of insurrection met firmly with an assertive discipline program. She commented, "Misconduct is a real problem. I've been working very hard on a new discipline program. Consequently the children have been very unhappy." The discipline program involved checks for misbehavior and an award of tokens for correct behavior. These tokens could be cashed in for small prizes. As part of her program to get the classroom under control, she also implemented a new schedule that would keep her students together on the same activity and moving at a faster pace, or so was her intent.

> I am structuring software activities that last approximately 20 minutes. They will have three changes of activities in the post-lunch hour. Typically, this hour has been most difficult to keep kids on task. The kids were asked to keep track of the 20-minute intervals. I feel the need for more structure.

She noted, however, a problem. One particular piece of software that she used in conjunction with social studies was very popular. This software, not the restrictive time schedule, was seen as the problem. As a result, some children were not permitted to use it. Meanwhile, she continued to report worsening discipline problems.

Experimenting Again

In late January, Mrs. Bennett again questioned her direction. Things were not going well. The classroom, she admitted, was not like it was in the past, and she needed a different kind of response from children to keep it working. She was once again drawn to think about students working together and taking more responsibility, and she began to open up her class once more.

> I will have to change some of the assertive discipline behavior plans that worked so well last year. Last year the children were not allowed to speak without raising their hands, and had to ask permission to leave their desks. But now the students are interacting with each other about their software. They are helping each other. I need this kind of cooperation.

Although Mrs. Bennett felt a need to change her approach to discipline, she still had trouble tolerating children leaving their seats. But when one child walked over to read a new chart on the bulletin board, she reported not having the heart to put the student's name on the board and take away her reward for the day. Mrs. Bennett's rigid adherence to her assertive discipline program faded away.

At the same time, her reports chronicled larger, more ambitious task designs for her students. Once again, she created opportunities for her students to work together for extended periods of time, and she gave them an increased choice of tools with which to work.

> Students searched for information on manufacturing goods in the mid-Atlantic states. They didn't finish during the class period. They had the option to use other programs. I was pleased to see that most kids chose to finish their database search. They really enjoy collecting information that way. The slow kids seem to enjoy it, too.

The class newspaper reappeared in her notes. Under the banner "Good Things Happen" she proclaimed progress, even though "noise"

still troubled her. Apparently, things were going so well that rem-
nants of "real school" began to bother Mrs. Bennett as much as
noise. She reported:

> The reading groups are my biggest pain. These groups interfere
> with computer activities. I wish there was some way to restructure
> the school day to avoid the 20-minute reading circles. There must
> be another way to teach reading.

Her enthusiasm for a different approach continued:

> Today I had an experience that I've never had before—everyone
> was on task. They had a task which required them to add -*est*
> extensions to words. Everybody was working merrily away.
> Brenda was sucking her thumb with one hand and typing with
> the other. That was quite funny. I asked a friend to video this
> because it had never happened before. The kids were just typing
> away. All you could hear was the sound of the typing keys. It was
> really wonderful.

These successes seemed to herald a new day for Mrs. Bennett. On the
same tape two additional episodes communicated a subtle change. In
the first, yet another opportunity for "commotion" appeared as her
students began to assert themselves. Where this might have been met
with strong resistance before, Mrs. Bennett seemed to step aside as
an observer and reflect that this latest development in student behavior might be a problem for other teachers:

> The kids like to print things. They like to print whatever is on the
> screen. There is competition to use the printers. Some of the kids
> have become self-appointed experts that oversee the printing of
> others. At times printing results in minor conflicts. Printing
> creates lots of commotion. Regular teachers will object to this.

In the second episode she even offered advice to future teachers
about "student freedoms," almost as if those freedoms were inalien-
able rights.

> Using the printers requires students to break out of regimented
> behavior patterns. They are not used to such freedoms, which
> creates lots of commotion. Teachers will have to train students to
> deal with these freedoms quite early.

Retiring from the ACOT Project

As illustrated by these entries, Mrs. Bennett vacillated all year between traditional approaches to instruction that had worked for years and new patterns of instruction that seemed somehow more appropriate in her technology-rich classroom. Her pedagogic swings resulted from inner conflict between how she believed classrooms should function, sound, and look and how she experienced instruction in a radically altered classroom, where students sat in front of computers and boxes of software. Her students were motivated to learn with those tools, and they had acquired a great deal of skill in doing so. The students themselves challenged old assumptions, not through insurrection but through steady pressure to work at those things that were enjoyable and useful. It was not easy for Mrs. Bennett to accept that old patterns no longer applied.

In fact, a cycle had been created. First Mrs. Bennett initiated an innovation that led to both intended and unintended outcomes. These unintended outcomes made her world more uncertain, raising her personal anxiety, and led her to question the basic premise on which she based her attempts to innovate. She reduced the dissonance by returning to behaviors that were consonant with her beliefs, but she then encountered resistance from her students, who preferred the more innovative activities to the traditional ones. Moving to reduce this source of dissonance, she would, again, attempt a more innovative path until her anxiety level rose once more. The process was exhausting for Mrs. Bennett and contributed to her retirement from the ACOT project after her first year.

In our second case study, Mrs. Lee follows a similar path, full of switchbacks between a tradition-bound, lecture-based curriculum and an individualized approach that benefited from spontaneous student collaboration. Her feelings and instructional behaviors pivoted as she tried to resolve the conflict between her conservative beliefs about learning and teaching and her own experiences with students in the peculiar, computer-filled classroom. Although she experienced similar setbacks, she did not leave the project. In fact, she seemed to return year after year with increasing pedagogical strength and certainty about her direction. Much of her success stemmed from the wealth of support and institutional resources at her school.

CHRISTINE LEE: NINTH- AND TENTH-GRADE MATH

Mrs. Lee taught mathematics in an urban high school located in a working-class community. Of the 1,300 students enrolled in the school, half are minorities. At this site a cohort of ACOT students worked with a team of teachers responsible for coursework in mathematics, science, social studies, and English. Mrs. Lee joined the project in its second year.

Observing Other ACOT Teachers

When she first began with ACOT, Mrs. Lee took time to observe a teacher who had worked with ACOT from its inception. She noted a difference from the traditional environments in which she had worked: "I watched the applications class and saw that I really have 30 teachers (students) in my class and I should use them." Despite her recognition of her students' skills, she worried for months about her lack of technical expertise and wondered what her students would think of her. It was hard to abandon the image of herself as the authority in her classroom.

> I'm uneasy about the kids' response to me when I'm working with the computers and don't really know what I'm doing . . . You wonder what the kids will think if they know more than you do. The students have never held their knowledge as a threat, and they are great at helping me. It's something in myself that I'm uncomfortable with in this situation.

She also noted that the technology brought its own set of issues, one of which challenged her beliefs about students doing their own work. It was an observation that made her less than enthusiastic about collaborative work, but one that would change radically in the coming years.

> I noticed that in the applications class students were exchanging disks, copying database work, and turning in the same work. Is cheating made easier by the computer?

From "Real School" to Risk Taking

She implemented what she knew best: a lecture-oriented program where new topics were presented and students took assignments home, returning the next day to have their work checked. But she was unhappy with the results: "The kids are bored. They're doing their homework from other subjects when I am teaching." In mid-December Mrs. Lee presented the students with an alternative to their diet of math lecture and recitation. The change brought an immediate, positive response from her students and opened Mrs. Lee to new ways of thinking about instruction.

> When I started showing the kids how to assemble their string art projects, I expected to have to explain it to each individual kid. What happened was that I explained it to one kid and then the rest got together and figured it out together. They're so used to working with each other that they don't hesitate to figure out assignments together. I've never seen this happen before. It was great to watch them work together.

Returning from winter break, Mrs. Lee continued to work more with small groups. Although she was generally pleased with students' progress, she had a difficult time shaking the feeling that she wasn't really teaching. The word "guilty" enters the record for the first, but not the last, time.

> I'm concerned about what's happening in Algebra and Geometry. When I try to be objective about it, I feel like I'm spending less time up there teaching. We now have disks for some lessons, which I refer the students to. I know they're learning very well with the computer . . . I feel a little guilty. It's a strange sensation.

Fewer lectures and more small-group assignments brought her closer to her students. The fact that she was closer to the action began to change her perspective on what happened when children put their heads together. Growing trust was followed by more risk taking.

> Today we just experimented with graphing and some other functions. It's the first time we've all just played with the software to see what it'll do. It was really rewarding because the kids and I were willing to experiment. Usually I want to know what's going to happen so I don't mess anything up or waste time.

By February there was an obvious shift in Mrs. Lee's attitude about group work. She had set out to change the way she taught, and she had also begun to glimpse the size of the task.

> I'll tell you, I feel like I'm not doing a good job. But it's all work on my part. I read the history of math every morning at breakfast and spend every free moment planning. There is so much more

> I want to do with my kids—to present lessons in a neat, experimental way.

She reflected on the results of her efforts and found problems but enough success to encourage her to continue. She justified an occasional lecture. She also examined her difficulty "letting loose of being the authority."

> My idea is to occasionally be the general instructor in the familiar and traditional way when that is appropriate, but I am interested in individualization. And I'm excited about it, but I'm hesitant about it. It's hard to let loose of being the authority, and that's what we're familiar with and the way we were taught.

Beliefs in Conflict

Mrs. Lee received a jolt from a substitute teacher, a retired veteran. New and old beliefs were once again placed in conflict.

> My team teacher was out with sick children today and they sent a substitute, which they don't usually do. He was a retired science teacher with a very different and serious attitude, and he commented that the classroom atmosphere was much too loose. I punished the one student that really talked out of turn, but the substitute made me wonder if we really were too nontraditional.

The sting of the criticism lasted for weeks and appeared in her account as fear, doubt, and, once again, guilt. But even in those expressions, another part of her argued for the collaborative, student-centered vision of teaching.

> I feel guilty when I let the students work in groups, for fear they will just play around. But they did a real good job today with their geometry projects on the computer in spite of the beautiful weather and the approaching spring vacation.

By the end of her first year in the project, Mrs. Lee had worked steadily at changing her instructional behavior, but nagging doubts persisted to the end.

> One thing I have had a hard time with as a traditional classroom teacher is to let them go, let the students try a new way. I find myself falling back into the old way because it's easier and saves

me time. Yet I'm not satisfied with lecturing to the students, and I really look forward to planning ways to take advantage of the alternative teaching styles available to me.

Linking Goals and Teaching Strategies

Mrs. Lee returned from summer vacation with a totally revamped math program. Over the break, she had worked with another math teacher to develop an individualized Algebra I, Algebra II, and Geometry curriculum that she would team teach with a new member of the ACOT staff. Her first report contrasted dramatically with the kids-who-work-together-must-be-cheating attitude that she had held at the beginning of the previous year.

> We started the individualized program today . . . I praised two students who were talking over the work between themselves, which surprised them. It is going to take a while to get across to the students how this goes.

But the very next day, she recorded the following comment about a critical incident:

> The program is going really well, but today I just got sick and tired of explaining the same thing 20 or 30 times, so I just stopped the geometry class and just lectured to everyone in geometry on the same questions that I was getting from everybody. It seemed to work out real well.

The success of this strategy led to renewed feelings of uncertainty about her instructional choices. Although lecture was appropriate under these circumstances, Mrs. Lee saw the two approaches, individualized versus teacher-directed instruction, as incompatible rather than complementary.

Later, with fresh energy, Mrs. Lee redoubled her efforts to change the norms of her classroom. By mid-December she was voicing a new confidence in her individualized, collaborative approach. One statement of that new confidence came as a reflection on her participation in a staff-development workshop:

> One question that occurred was, "Don't students cheat and look at each other's screens?" I defended the students' looking at each others work. They learn by seeing what others are doing and I encouraged peer interaction and peer group work. They thought

that was interesting because they haven't used the computers enough to realize this . . . I pointed out that it takes a while for students and teachers to learn that students can work together, because we are used to the traditional classroom. I was preaching in favor of the things that I was hesitant about on individualized study. I do not have to be in front of the class at all times. It made everything gel for me, and I was pleased with that.

The next week she made the following entry in her log:

I think about the way I taught in the old days, three years ago. Lecture, summarize, give examples and assign homework. In each class the students only worked on problems at home and then came back with questions, which I would ask for at the beginning of the period. I dreaded the routine. I loved test days when I didn't have to do anything. I think about how differently I do things now, with ACOT and the individualized program. I could not go back to the old way. I will always keep this individualization with me, even if I went back to a regular classroom. Many kids can learn on their own, and many can take responsibility for instruction. I am seeing their capabilities as I have never seen them before.

Mrs. Lee began fine tuning her approach. She looked for ways to combine the best that she had known from her traditional days with her new goals. Overall, she reported success after success.

They all got 100%! So the review session they had amongst themselves must have been unbelievable, and it didn't even take them longer than 15 minutes. It is so exciting to see that these kids can learn from each other, that they don't have to have a teacher standing over them at all times. I'm overwhelmed, but on the other hand, they're learning without my help, and it's a little [bit] of a shock to get over.

One last entry illustrates that old patterns emerge again and again, even after continued success with new behaviors. Their appearance surprises even the perpetrator. The following is taken from Mrs. Lee's journal after two years in the project:

I lectured and summarized and felt like I was talking to a wall. It's interesting how I go back to a straight lecture situation, after the kids have been involved in so many group activities and getting their brain cells to work during class, and all of a sudden they just sit there like vegetables. It's yucky to see them sitting there looking at me.

THE INFLUENCE OF CONTEXT ON INSTRUCTIONAL CHANGE

These cases show two teachers in different settings striving to change their instructional approaches to fit their technology-rich classrooms. However, there was a significant difference in the contexts in which these two teachers strived to change. Not all district, school, or personal contexts support risk taking. Mrs. Bennett taught in a traditionally organized elementary school; she worked in a self-contained classroom with little to no opportunity to watch other teachers or even discuss what she was attempting to do. She viewed the ACOT coordinator at her site more like an evaluator than a colleague with whom to share ideas, successes, and failures. As the only classroom teacher involved in the ACOT project at her school, she felt isolated and believed that colleagues and administrators were critical of her efforts. Other teachers developed hostility toward the project, focusing on the incoming resources from Apple Computer rather than the huge investment of time and effort by Mrs. Bennett. In an effort to lessen the tension, the principal began to reapportion other school resources, such as library time and paper, to other classrooms, reducing resources for the ACOT classroom. Mrs. Bennett felt outraged that her students were essentially being locked out of the library.

At the district level, the project became a "political football." Decision-making power about and credit for the ACOT project continued to be debated between the school principal and district personnel. While an area superintendent believed she had ultimate responsibility for the project, the principal viewed the project as taking place at her school, thus making her in charge. In addition, the district strictly adhered to the state's emphasis on mastery of basic skills, and administrators felt strongly committed to raising students' test scores. In this context, Mrs. Bennett naturally felt increasingly stressed rather than supported.

Instead of easing her stress, her personal situation compounded it. The daily requirements of integrating technology into her classroom led her to spend more hours at school and at home in the evenings and on weekends working on school-related tasks. These new demands competed with her family responsibilities. In addition, her family witnessed her emotional ups and downs as she came home with stories of success and failure. Concerned about the time demands and the emotional toll, her family eventually encouraged her to discontinue her participation in the project.

In contrast, Mrs. Lee entered the ACOT project in its second year at her high school. The first-year staff had established strongly held values about joint planning, team teaching, and interdisciplinary instruction. Mrs. Lee, by the nature of her context, had constant opportunity to watch other teachers in action and to talk with them informally throughout the day. The team of teachers were constantly in and out of each other's classrooms, helping to solve problems and lending support. At the school level, the principal took a number of steps to establish the program as part of the larger school culture. For example, she countered the issue of "the haves and the have-nots" by helping teachers think about other intensive innovations going on the building. In addition, she provided time for interested teachers to visit the ACOT classrooms. She also designed opportunities for other teachers to use the technology in the school. In the early years, the ACOT teachers also taught non-ACOT classes, giving them plenty of occasions to interact with colleagues on other projects.

The district context added an additional layer of support for Mrs. Lee. There was no political tension between the district and the school regarding the project, and the district technology coordinator was a former math teacher who could relate to Mrs. Lee's efforts. She visited the school frequently, enthusiastically offering help and support. Both the principal and the district technology coordinator routinely praised the program and its direction.

Although Mrs. Lee also found that the project required additional time at school and at home, her personal situation made it easier to spend the time without jeopardizing her family relationships. Clearly, the district, school, and personal contexts in which Mrs. Lee worked provided the support she needed to engage in intensive innovation and risk taking.

Instructional innovation involves not just change in people but also changes in organizational culture. Teachers bold enough to participate in these efforts require and deserve modifications in their organizations' structure: alterations that permit and encourage peer observation, dialogue, and reflection. Most importantly, they must gain continued assurance that their struggles are worthwhile. In the first setting, Mrs. Bennett succumbed to the sheer weight of her efforts; in the second, Mrs. Lee flourished, despite periodic setbacks.

While teachers are in the thick of change, confronting their beliefs, the context becomes increasingly important. In addition to illustrating contextual influences, these two teachers' stories suggest that movement from one belief system to another is not orderly, uni-directional, or, perhaps, ever final. Yet the experiences of the ACOT teachers as a group depict an overall direction of instructional evolution. The next chapter describes the stages included in this evolutionary process.

3

The Evolution of Instruction in Technology-Rich Classrooms

"" *One thing I have a hard time with as a traditional classroom teacher is to let them go, let the students try a new way.* ""

The stories of Mrs. Bennett and Mrs. Lee portray two individuals' struggles to integrate technology into the classroom. Although individual ACOT teachers' experiences differed in many ways, when we looked across the project as a whole, commonalities became evident. While the sheer number of computers in ACOT classrooms quickly and radically transformed physical space and altered student and teacher expectations about what might occur, other aspects, such as the nature of classroom interactions, student work, and teacher roles, changed at a much slower pace. Gradually, new patterns of teaching and learning emerged at all sites. There seemed to be a predictable flow, a staged progression over time similar to other models of educational change (e.g., Berman & McLaughlin, 1976; Giacquinta, 1973; Gross & Herriott, 1979).

Our model, which is described in this chapter, provides a road map for teachers just beginning to use technology in their classrooms. Successive generations of ACOT teachers and those who participated in the ACOT Teacher Development Center project benefited from learning about this model since it gave them ideas about what direction they were headed, what they might expect, and what milestones they could observe to gauge their progress. While it is unlikely that any two teachers will ever progress at the same rate and in the same way through these stages, knowing that other teachers followed this route may provide the confidence necessary to minimize the two-steps-forward, one-step-backward behavior that characterized the professional development of Mrs. Bennett and Mrs. Lee.

In this chapter we discuss why technology is not a panacea for educational reform and examine the influence of personal beliefs on innovation. Then we describe the stages in our model of instructional evolution and, finally, identify ways to support the integration of technology into classrooms.

THE PROMISE OF TECHNOLOGY FOR EDUCATION

In the early days of the introduction of computers to classrooms, there was unbridled hope that technology would bring about the same kind of successful transformation that had been seen in science, industry, and business. In these arenas, technology's role seemed obvious from the start. In science, automated computation allowed measurement and comparisons never before possible. Simulations made whole classes of natural phenomena accessible and opened them to experimentation. In industry, repetitious and well-specified processes suggested computerized and roboticized solutions, eliminating the errors and hazards that come with human boredom. In business, the flexibility of the word processor over the typewriter was immediately obvious. In each of these fields, clear procedures combined with technology led to quantum leaps in efficiency.

Technology's role in schooling is not so obvious, in part because the process and product of formal education remain largely unspecified. Learning and teaching may be the fundamental processes of schooling, but perspectives on learning are constantly changing and images of teaching vary widely (Greene, 1979). Some argue that teaching is a clinical pursuit, where practitioners control instructional variables (Smith, 1963). Others view it as an enterprise, where teachers create learning communities and focus on social processes (Dewey, 1963). Or, to some, the practice of teaching might be more like therapy, where a teacher recognizes unique moments that present students with opportunities for growth and capitalizes on them (Buber, 1957). None of these images of teaching has proven superior to any other. To some extent, they all coexist in schools today.

Learning outcomes are equally subject to debate. Witness the raucous clash over educational standards. What are they, and who should define them? Should standards be set by local, state, or national groups? Should parents, professional educators, policymakers, or business and industry leaders drive the process? How do you factor in conservative and liberal perspectives or religious and secular interests? How do you account for regional differences?

Adding more complexity to this picture, children arrive at classroom doors in countless shades of physical, emotional, social, and cognitive readiness. Still, teachers greet their students year after year and attempt to help them develop their intellectual and emotional potential and provide some sense of greater purpose and social responsibility. No wonder that school reformers responded optimistically to the introduction of educational technology. At some level, perhaps, dealing with hardware and software seemed so much simpler than contending with issues as complex as human cognition, politics, and values.

When computers were first introduced to classrooms, reformers focused on the innovation—computers and software. They gave little thought to how technology would integrate into instruction and influence assessment. In many ways, ACOT repeated the same error. The addition of large numbers of computers, peripherals, and software to ACOT classrooms did catalyze change, but their contribution was clearly mediated by familiar human, organizational, and educational issues. Technology by itself was not the silver bullet. In fact, it added yet another layer of complexity, a whole new set of things for already overworked and stressed teachers to learn and manage. Yet, as the project continued, teachers found strategic ways to use the technology. Its use in instruction and learning changed as teachers themselves changed. The speed and direction of this evolution were closely tied to changes in teachers' beliefs about learning, about teacher-student roles, and about instructional practice.

THE IMPORTANCE OF PERSONAL BELIEFS TO INSTRUCTIONAL EVOLUTION

Beliefs play an important part in human endeavors, particularly in situations where there is a great deal of uncertainty, as in schools (Nespor, 1987). Beliefs are personal and are individually derived, they form the basis for individuals' perspectives about right and wrong, and they predispose individuals to certain modes of conduct (Rokeach, 1975). From a cultural perspective, the potency and permanence of beliefs are greatly heightened when groups share common beliefs (Schein, 1985). Teachers enter the profession with deeply held notions about how to conduct school—they teach as they were taught. If these beliefs are commonly held and help teachers negotiate the uncertainty of work in schools, no wonder teachers are reticent to adopt practices that have not stood the test of time. If beliefs govern behavior, the process of replacing old beliefs with new becomes critically important in changing educational practice in schools. Schein describes how beliefs are replaced in groups:

> When a group faces a new task, issue, or problem . . . someone in the group, usually the founder, has convictions about the nature of reality and how to deal with it, and will propose a solution based on those convictions . . . If the solution works, and the group has a shared perception of success . . . group members will tend to forget that originally they were not sure and that the values were therefore debated and confronted. As the values begin to be taken for granted, they gradually become beliefs and assumptions and drop out of consciousness, just as habits become unconscious and automatic. (p. 15–16)

This perspective explains the approach-avoidance behavior of both Mrs. Bennett and Mrs. Lee as they struggled to integrate technology into their daily activities with students. Replacing old teaching habits took time and repeated success. It also required recognition from their peers and administrators that they were being successful with new practices and technology. New beliefs were reluctantly forged.

Schein's perspective about how beliefs are replaced in groups helped us understand the significance of the changes we watched unfold across the entire project. In the next section, we look at patterns of teaching and learning that emerged over time and describe our conceptual framework through the stories of ACOT teachers' classroom experiences.

STAGES OF INSTRUCTIONAL EVOLUTION

Our model includes five stages: entry, adoption, adaptation, appropriation, and invention. In this model, text-based curriculum delivered in a lecture–recitation–seat work mode is first strengthened through the use of technology and then gradually replaced by far more dynamic learning experiences for students.

Entry

At the time the project began, an instructional technology already existed in each of the ACOT classrooms. This technology was text based, and the common tools were blackboards, textbooks, workbooks, ditto sheets, and overhead projectors. These tools were used in combination to support lecture, recitation, and seat work. "Real school," as described in Chapter 1, was firmly in place. Teachers who were beginning with the project had little or no experience with computer technology and were in various stages of trepidation and excitement. At each site, teachers spent the first weeks of the project unpacking boxes, running extension cords, untangling cables, inserting cards, formatting disks, checking out home computers, and generally trying to establish order in radically transformed physical environments.

During this unavoidable initiation, experienced teachers found themselves facing problems typical of first-year teachers: discipline, resource management, and the personal frustration that comes from making time-consuming mistakes in already crowded days (see Chapter 4). Their audiotape journals were full of comments that expressed serious reservations about students' access to computers and about whether the new technology would ever "fit in." One of the project's elementary teachers commented, "There's too much fooling around with the computer—mousing around—when students are supposed to be listening." Another noted:

> Time is always going to be a problem. Teachers need help just to get equipment up and running sometimes. I do not seem to have enough time to meet the needs of everyone. I keep up by going in on weekends to complete the technical work.

Occasionally, ACOT teachers had second thoughts about the wisdom of their mission. After a number of months, however, equipment was finally in place, and teachers and students had mastered the technology basics. With more certainty about simple technical matters, there was less concern about time, and teachers began to focus again on instruction, the signal that they had entered a new phase, which we call adoption.

Adoption

While technology issues for ACOT teachers were far from over during the adoption stage, teachers—in their conversations, weekly reports, and audiotape journals—showed more concern about how technology could be integrated into daily instructional plans. Interspersed among traditional whole-group lectures, recitations, and seat work, teachers incorporated computer-based activities aimed primarily at teaching children how to use technology. Keyboarding instruction, for example, got under way at all of the sites. It typically occurred in 15-minute increments for a six-week period; at the end of this time, even eight-year-olds were typing 18–20 words per minute. Training on how to use word processors was a common next step, progressing in all instances far faster than teachers imagined. For example, high school teachers developed a multiweek unit on word processing. Instead of students taking weeks, teachers found students rushing ahead through feature after feature on their own and mastering the use of the software in a few hours over a number of days. Another common instructional agenda was learning how to save, store, and organize work.

At the elementary level, teachers spent inordinate amounts of time evaluating any of the hundreds of software programs that were available at that time for the Apple IIe computer, searching for just the right content and approach for a specific lesson. High school teachers, because they had chosen to work with Macintosh computers, skipped the time-consuming step of software evaluation; there simply were no educational software programs available at that early point in the Macintosh development. Consequently, sooner than their elementary colleagues, the ACOT high school teachers investigated other tool-based software such as databases, graphics programs, and spreadsheets for use in their classrooms. But in both instances, the teachers searched for software they could adapt to their established curricular and pedagogical preferences. Although much had changed physically in the classrooms, more remained the same.

With hindsight, there is little surprise that change was not faster and more dramatic. Given their lack of experience with the technology, teachers attempted to blend its use into the most familiar form of classroom practice, direct instruction. There were, in the beginning of the program, no successful experiences powerful enough to displace more comfortable patterns of operating. In addition to teachers' internal reticence, external forces influenced their instruction as well. At the high school site, an observer hired by the district noted the heavy emphasis on the official course of study and just how little leeway teachers perceived they had in varying from that guide (Damarin & Bohren, 1987). The same was true at the elementary sites, where teachers felt pressure to make sure their students would perform well on standardized tests of basic skills. At two elementary sites, annual teacher evaluations created concern. Would district observers allow for messier, noisier classrooms where children were not necessarily all doing the same things at the same time? Parents, too, voiced their concerns: "Will my child's handwriting develop naturally?" and "Will they do anything with this technology other than play games?" Teachers were very aware of the contextual constraints in which they worked.

Given frequent disruptions to normal classroom operation that came with beginning attempts to use the computers, we anticipated short-term declines in student performance in the adoption stage. Traditional measures of achievement, however, showed no significant decline or improvement in student performance aggregated at the classroom level (Baker, Herman, & Gearhart, 1989). Teachers reported that individual students performed better and were more motivated. What we witnessed during this period was the adoption of the new electronic technology to support text-based drill-and-practice instruction. ACOT staff hoped for more and began to see it in the next stage of teachers' progress with technology—adaptation.

Adaptation

In this phase, the new technology became thoroughly integrated into traditional classroom practice. Lecture, recitation, and seat work remained the dominant form of student tasks; but students used word processors, databases, some graphic programs, and many computer-assisted-instructional (CAI) packages for approximately 30–40% of the school day. More frequent and purposeful use of technology began to return dividends.

Productivity emerged as a major theme. Teachers reported that their students produced more and at a faster rate. In a self-paced, computational math program, for example, sixth-grade students completed the year's curriculum by the beginning of April, creating a quandary of what to do in math for the remainder of the year. The mere suggestion that these children start the seventh-grade math curriculum early created an uproar among seventh-grade teachers: "What will we do when we get the children next fall?" The solution was to use the balance of the year to focus the sixth-graders on application and problem solving. A revelation to the teachers was that students who were not usually enamored of math and rarely performed well became engaged in the hands-on, problem-solving approach. These students then became recognized as creative math-problem solvers. In future years, teachers at this site assigned most of the more traditional computational math activities as homework to be completed on the home computers and used class time for application and problem-solving activities.

At an elementary site, teachers focused on basic math and language-arts skills and used their computers purposefully to raise student test scores. For two years in a row the district reported that ACOT students scored significantly higher on the California Achievement Test than non-ACOT students in vocabulary, reading comprehension, language mechanics, math computation, and math concepts and application (Memphis Public Schools, 1987). At other sites, which were less focused on basic skill development, teachers still expressed fears that time spent on developing technology skills (rather than on covering the standard curriculum) might erode student test scores. Less time spent on basics, however, did not have a negative impact on student performance on tests at these sites (Baker, Herman, & Gearhart, 1989).

The productivity theme emerged at the high school level as well. In chemistry, students learned to use a simple graphics program to illustrate molecules and the exchange of atoms in chemical reactions.

As a result, the teacher reported that students learned how to write and balance chemical formulas faster and more accurately than in his previous experience. As he explained, "It is great to be able to compress lesson time because of the software tools we now have." The chemistry teacher's supervisor also noted a change in the efficiency of the instructional process:

> The students have access to the total assignment on the network and are working through it much more quickly and with more understanding. Many of them never use paper and pencil on the assignment at all. They download the teacher's handouts to their computers, work on the tasks assigned, and send the final copy of their work to the printer to be picked up by the teacher. No more pages and pages of handouts that are lost, replaced, and lost again.

Writing was another area that drew frequent comment from the sites in the adaptation phase. A weekly report from a fourth-grade classroom read:

> I was amazed at the speed at which some of the students could use the word processor. I have noticed that increasingly this word-processing program has become the preferred manner of preparing assignments. Many of the students can now type faster than they can write.

A special education teacher reported:

> Students are writing with a great deal more fluency now, thanks to keyboarding skills. Following a prewriting exercise, they now type their stories directly into the computer, rather than writing out the whole story and then copying it.

Researchers who examined writing in one third-grade ACOT classroom determined that children maintained a high level of enthusiasm for and interest in writing during the six-month study; that computers made compositions more presentable to others, thus encouraging writing; and that students wrote more and better as a function of the accessibility of computers (Hiebert, Quellmalz, & Vogel, 1987). Increased productivity in writing led to a bounty of text that allowed teachers to work with even young students on narrative skills. Willingly, students reworked their papers, a rare occurrence in paper-and-pencil classrooms. The same outpouring of text over-whelmed the project teachers and led to the need for new strategies for instruction, feedback, and evaluation.

During the adaptation phase, teachers also noted changes in the quality of student engagement in classroom tasks. The following reports from elementary sites are representative of those observations. As one teacher described:

> On Monday, when I announced that it was time for recess, the students wanted to continue to work in the classroom. One said, "You know, I can't believe it's really recess. When you're having a good time, time goes by so fast." They are really involved . . . They work really quietly without a lot of running around. They seem to be setting up standards for themselves to judge their own work.

Another teacher noted:

> This class is made up of children who had difficulty with the third grade and were not quite ready for the fourth. They are easily distracted . . . They are less inclined to get off task when working on the computer and less intimidated with math problems than when working from a book.

In addition, teachers reported that students were increasingly more curious and assertive learners in the technology-rich classrooms, taking on new challenges far beyond the normal assignments (Fisher, 1991).

Appropriation

Appropriation is less a phase in instructional evolution and more a milestone.[1] It is evidenced less by change in classroom practice and more by change of personal attitude toward technology. It comes with teachers' personal mastery of the technologies they are attempting to employ in their classes. Appropriation is the point at which an individual comes to understand technology and use it effortlessly as a tool to accomplish real work. Perhaps it is best described in the

1. In earlier descriptions of appropriation (e.g., Dwyer, Ringstaff, & Sandholtz, 1991), we discussed appropriation as a stage in the evolutionary process and included much of the description of interdisciplinary and project-based activities in the classrooms in it. In retrospect, we want to emphasize the personal nature of appropriation and assign the classroom shifts to the invention stage.

words of two ACOT teachers. The first teacher is on the doorstep of appropriation:

> I'm still getting more confident in my use of computers. Seems that my day unconsciously revolves around the use of computers. I do lesson plans, notes and correspondence, report card information, history information, current events—all on the computer. I appreciate how it lets me function better as a teacher, when it's working. I don't think it's more important than any other teaching tool. However, it has a wide variety of uses.

The second teacher has crossed the threshold:

> Last spring, when I was taking a course at the university, I borrowed a computer and I did my whole term paper on it. I could not believe how labor saving it was, and now I believe, like many other teachers who have discovered the same thing, that it would be hard to live without a computer. If you had to take the computer I have at home, I would have to go out and buy one. I would have to have a computer. It has become a way of life.

The teachers' comments underscore the process of replacing old habits with new. When individuals have a shared perception of success, they forget their original doubts and their new values gradually become beliefs that are taken for granted (Schein, 1985). Teachers' new habits reveal a change in beliefs about the usefulness of technology. This milestone is a necessary and critical step before one can move onto more imaginative uses of technology for teaching and learning.

In the pioneering days of the ACOT project, few teachers in the world, much less their students, had enough access to technology to truly appropriate it (Becker, 1987; Office of Technology Assessment, 1988). In our view, lack of access to technology and little opportunity for appropriation underlie much of the criticism about technology use in schools. Teachers are simply unable to move on to more innovative uses and demonstrate new kinds of outcomes for students. Computers remain tools for efficiency, an underwhelming justification for their broader deployment (Cuban, 1986). Appropriation is the turning point for teachers—the end of efforts simply to computerize their traditional practice. It leads to the next stage, invention, where new teaching approaches promote the basics yet open the possibility of a new set of student competencies.

Invention

> I was so excited after the first day, I thought it was too good to be true. The students were using page layout software to make a publication in a 40-minute class period using the network . . . All students saved and quit within three minutes before the bell. It runs like a charm . . . Now we can simulate a newspaper company. Eventually, students will work in groups, each with their own task, some for art, business graphs, articles, and the editing group. Students can place finished work on a public share disk for the editing group to retrieve and complete the publication.

One of ACOT's high school teachers had developed so much confidence with networking technology and a professional page layout program that he ignored company warnings that his plan would never work. Guided by a vision of an ambitious writing project that would engage his students in a highly collaborative and creative activity, he doggedly continued until he succeeded. That success opened the way to an annual publication of students' writing that became as important to them as their yearbook at graduation. This is one example of what happens beyond appropriation.

In the invention stage, teachers experimented with new instructional patterns and ways of relating to students and to other teachers. As more teachers reached this stage, the whole tenor of the sites began to change. Interdisciplinary project-based instruction, team teaching, and individually paced instruction became common. Students were busier, more active; the classrooms buzzed.

At the high school site, students and teachers joined in a study of the renovation effort under way in their own city's business and government center. They began to design a large-scale model of the downtown, animated with robotics and controlled by a dozen or more computers. The final construction sat on a 10-by-20-foot base and incorporated 4-foot-tall models of buildings complete in every detail. A weekly electronic memo shared among all the ACOT sites described the project in progress in its late stages:

> The district art teacher will be with the ACOT students the entire six periods Monday as they put their model of the city together. The applications teacher has conned the rest of the team into giving up their classes so the students can have a full day of Computer Applications . . . This has been a wonderful, integrated

activity for students. They are using the robotics they have to build parts of our city . . . The students researched the actual height of the buildings downtown and followed that by doing the mathematical proportions that must be done to determine the heights and widths of the model building accurately.

The success of this first big event led to subsequent projects the next school year, including an embellished return of the city project that included field trips to specific buildings and research about the individuals and businesses that occupied them.

At both the elementary and secondary levels, this type of teamed, project-based learning activity created opportunities for teachers to step back and observe their students. They saw their students' highly evolved skill with technology, their ability to learn on their own, and their movement away from competitive work patterns toward collaborative ones. For example, one teacher said:

> It's amazing to me how much these kids are learning . . . Kids are doing things that are not assigned. The excitement is that they are motivated, seeing the power of the things which they are learning how to use, creating for themselves solutions to problems for other things. That is the goal of the educator. That the student be motivated to solve problems important to him, not to go after points. You never see this in regular classes.

Another teacher, describing a project in which students designed a calculator using a hypermedia application, reported:

> It was just so gratifying to see that as soon as one student finished, they would go look at another student's, saying, "How did you get it to do that?" They shared strategies. "Didn't you do the extra credit?" "You know how to do square root? Let me show you." It was just that sort of give and take, that sort of excitement, contagious enthusiasm, high level of engagement that makes me feel that this really is a good model for the classroom of the future.

In yet another classroom, a teacher reflected on changes in the students' interactions:

> I tried to stand back today and take an overall view of what our classroom looks like. Some students were working on the board

with each other in small groups. Sue was working with Joe; they've never worked together before. Joe's mother has talked to me because she's upset that he's not succeeding in the math part of our program. One of his problems is that he is so shy; he just won't ask questions. So, Sue was helping Joe and he seemed to be understanding . . . I went and asked if she needed help. As soon as I left, I noticed Joe sought her out again for help. I thought, Wow, this is something that would not happen in a traditional high school math classroom.

Students helped other students over hurdles with the technology, and they helped their teachers. Some teachers were a bit defensive at first about their students' growing expertise, but they later adapted to the more empowered status of students (see Chapter 5).

Others noted changes as well. An independent observer studying one of the elementary sites commented on changes in communication patterns and on the extent of collaborative work among even the youngest students. She reported that the children interacted differently at the computers. They talked to each other more, frequently asked for assistance from their neighbors, quickly interrupted their own work to help someone else, and displayed tremendous curiosity about what others were doing (Phelan, 1989). A district technology supervisor at the high school site, observing the extent of peer interaction in the ACOT classroom, noted that by allowing students to teach each other, teachers' roles were changing as well.

The students really enjoy these group activities and, as we all know, learn more since they are actively rather than passively participating in the learning experience. Our teachers are learning to be facilitators rather than the total dispensers of knowledge. Everyone benefits.

The most important change in this phase was an increasing tendency of the ACOT teachers to reflect on teaching, to question old patterns, and to speculate about the causes behind changes they were seeing in their students. At the beginning of her third year with the project, one of ACOT's high school English teachers recorded in her audiotape journal: "It is all individualized and there is such a businesslike hum going on; there is such a good feel to it. It seems like what schools ought to be."

These types of changes in the learning environment benefited students. For instance, a longitudinal study of ACOT students at a high school site showed considerable differences when compared with their non-ACOT peers. ACOT students' absentee rate was 50%

less, and they had no dropouts, compared with the school's 30% rate. Although half of the students who joined ACOT as freshmen had not planned to go to college, 90% of them graduated and went on to college compared with 15% for the non-ACOT graduates. Moreover, this ACOT graduating class amassed 27 academic awards in addition to recognitions for outstanding accomplishments in history, calculus, foreign language, and writing.[2] The greatest difference in these students, however, was the manner in which they organized for and accomplished their work. They routinely employed inquiry, collaborative, technological, and problem-solving skills uncommon to graduates of traditional high school programs (Tierney, Kieffer, Whalin, Desai, & Gale, 1992). These skills are remarkably similar to competencies argued for by the U.S. Department of Labor (Secretary's Commission on Achieving Necessary Skills [SCANS], 1991). This report maintains that in addition to basic language and computational literacy, high school graduates must master the abilities to organize resources; work with others; locate, evaluate, and use information; understand complex work systems; and work with a variety of technologies.

The invention stage is the climax in the evolution of teachers' instructional strategies and beliefs. In ACOT's research, most, but not all, teachers reached this new plateau as classroom leaders. They demonstrated their comfort with a new set of beliefs about teaching and learning that was not common among teachers at the project's outset. Though there was variation, the ACOT teachers became more disposed to view learning as an active, creative, and socially interactive process than when they entered the program. Knowledge came to be viewed more as something that children must construct for themselves and less as something that can be transferred intact.

Reaching the invention stage, however, was a slow and arduous process for most teachers. In the following section, we describe the types of supports that can help teachers as they progress through the evolutionary stages.

BUILDING SUPPORT FOR INSTRUCTIONAL CHANGE

Technology is a catalyst for change in classroom processes because it provides a distinct departure, a change in context that suggests alternative

2. This graduating class was not a technical random sample of the high school students. We believe, however, that it was representative of the school as a whole. The magnitude of difference between the ACOT students' performance and that of their peers is provocative. Moreover, we have seen similar outcomes in subsequent graduating classes.

ways of operating. It can drive a shift from a traditional instructional approach toward a more eclectic set of learning activities that include knowledge-building situations for students. In this chapter, we discussed five common stages in that transition, highlighting changes in teachers' actions, in the way they employed technology at each stage, and in the resulting transformations in their students' work. Underlying this model is our view that such changes will occur only if there is a concomitant change in teachers' beliefs about their practice. However, instructional evolution is not simply a matter of abandoning beliefs but one of gradually replacing them with more relevant ones shaped by experiences in an altered context. Beliefs are a source of guidance in times of uncertainty; they are important in defining teaching tasks and organizing relevant information. They are an irreplaceable element in the process of imagining alternative futures—"envisioning and trying to establish instructional formats or systems of classroom relations of which there is no direct personal experience" (Nespor, 1987, p. 319).

The idea that deeply held beliefs are pivotal to change in practice frequently emerges in educational research (Baldridge & Deal, 1975; Chin & Benne, 1961; Cuban, 1986; Fullan, 1982; Giacquinta, 1973; Paul, 1977). However, the challenge lies in finding ways to help teachers confront their instructional beliefs.

Contextual Forms of Support

What can be done to foster the generation of values and attitudes that support innovations? Two conditions seem essential. First, before teachers can reflect on their beliefs, they must somehow bring them to a conscious level, and they must see and understand the connection between their beliefs and their actions. They must also be aware of alternative belief systems and experience positive consequences of those alternatives. Second, administrators must be willing to implement structural or programmatic shifts in the context or working environments of teachers who are instructionally evolving.

The process of change in ACOT classrooms involved more than introducing the technology and waiting for change to occur. Certain aspects of the project, such as data collection requirements and close working relationships among teachers and project researchers, gave teachers opportunities for reflection, which promoted changes in their personal beliefs about instruction. In addition, institutional and project supports altered the teachers' working environments.

At the same time that teachers transformed the structure of their classrooms, ACOT staff worked closely with school and district administrators to change the larger context in which the teachers worked. Institutional supports, including technical training on the use of hardware and software, and release time for collaboration and team planning, became routine for project teachers. Teachers also had opportunities to attend or present at professional conferences and to participate in workshops on instructional issues in which they expressed interest.

At each site, coordinators provided ongoing technical and instructional support. Whenever possible, administrators permitted daily schedules to be flexible, allowing for peer observation and team teaching. Teachers and coordinators also had access to a telecommunications network—linking participants, ACOT staff, researchers, and other educators. Teachers frequently used the network to discuss instructional issues, provide emotional support, and share experiences with participants at other sites (see Chapter 7). These forms of contextual support promoted change by decreasing teacher isolation. As teachers grappled with difficult instructional issues, they found it helpful to discuss their concerns with others in similar situations:

> James commented at our meeting that he is not comfortable at all with having the students work together. I felt uncomfortable with that last year, but ACOT has broken me away from that feeling, realizing that they can be very productive being instructional aides to each other. We pointed out to James that in our program if a student is having another student do their work for them, it's going to show on the test. Unlike the normal classroom, they can't just take their F and go on.

Opportunities for teacher reflection complemented these contextual changes and further promoted teacher change. The process of reflection helped teachers to see for themselves the benefits and drawbacks of different instructional approaches. Unlike many programs aimed at educational reform, this project provided built-in mechanisms that cultivated teacher reflection over the long term. For example, the data collection strategy requiring teachers to complete audiotapes provoked their analysis of classroom experiences. Although some teachers grumbled about the time necessary to comply with this requirement, many recognized the value of the exercise:

> These tape requirements that you have given us were the pits at first. Now I am really into them as a means of mental release . . . Anyhow, I'll stop beating around the bush. My tape recorder is broken. I now have nothing to talk into every day and I am feeling very panicky. Is there any way you could bring a new tape recorder to the conference? I would really appreciate it.

The process of completing weekly reports about major events and developments, which were telecommunicated to other sites, gave teachers further opportunities to reflect upon their teaching.

Another research component of the project involved having individual teachers work closely with university-based investigators on issues such as student empowerment, multimedia instruction, and mathematics software. Once again, teachers sometimes complained about the time they had to commit to these activities, but they also acknowledged that working closely with researchers had important benefits:

> This experiment with Cornell University is really forcing me to think through my thought processes about what I am doing and questions I am asking. It is really good and healthy for me to experience these challenges. I feel I am growing and learning more about myself, and becoming more aware of what is happening in the classroom.

Not only did working closely with researchers increase the opportunities for teachers to confront their own beliefs about teaching and learning, but it also validated their efforts to change:

> Working with researchers lets me know that I am not doing such a bad job, that I do come up with some good questions, and that I am becoming more secure about myself as I become more experienced at using a new teaching approach.

Similarly, periodic visitors to the classrooms provided an important audience for ACOT teachers. The visitors served as a source of valuable feedback, increasing teachers' reflections on their practices and reinforcing their experimentation with new methods. Being constantly observed by colleagues, particularly those from other schools, reemphasized the importance and value of their innovative strategies. Moreover, the changes teachers made in their instructional techniques were pervasive enough to be noted over time, rather than being temporary alterations meant to impress occasional visitors.

Incremental Steps to Altering Contexts

Recognizing that change is evolutionary, we suggest an incremental approach to altering contexts and providing needed supports. Table 3.1 delineates the kinds of training, activities, and support that parallel our five stages and can help expedite teachers' passage through them.

In the early stages of implementing technology in classrooms, teachers' needs center around their concerns over the technology itself: central processing units, disk drives, software, and other peripherals. Technical training, therefore, is a key ingredient that can reduce stress and boost confidence. But it will remain an isolated exercise, soon forgotten, unless it is situated in a context with purpose. As teachers learn technological basics, they need to be immersed in an environment that builds the links between technology and instruction and learning. They must have enough access to technology for themselves and for their students to make the exercise relevant. We also hold that teachers will more likely be successful if they engage in this process as volunteers and as members of teams. The first serious organizational shift comes with the need to schedule time for teams to meet routinely. Besides providing technology, allowing teachers time to acquire skills and assist one another is a clear indicator of any administrators' seriousness about this form of change.

We recommend forms of support for teacher change that are increasingly interactive as teachers progress through the evolutionary stages and that expand to include more and more teachers, mentors, and even researchers. Teachers need increased and varied opportunities to see other teachers, to confront their actions and examine their motives, and to reflect critically on the consequences of their choices, decisions, and actions. They need opportunities for ongoing dialogue about their experiences and for continuous development of their abilities to imagine and discover more powerful learning experiences for their students. Finally, both for teachers' own personal affirmation as well as for the creation of bodies of craft knowledge to support novice teachers, we recommend that teachers

Table 3.1 Support for instructional evolution in technology-rich classrooms

Phase	Expectation	Support
Entry	Volunteer team	Provide routine planning time to develop shared vision and practice
	Critical mass of technology present for teachers and students	Excuse staff from as many district requirements as possible
		Create opportunities for staff to share experiences with nonparticipant colleagues
Adoption	Keyboarding	Provide nuts-and-bolts technical support to develop teacher's confidence and ability to maintain hardware and facilitate children's use
	Use of word processors for writing	
	Use of CAI (computer-assisted instruction) software for drill and practice of basic skills	Provide CAI, keyboarding, and word-processing software and training
Adaptation	Many basic instructional activities individualized and self-paced	Develop flexible schedule to permit peer observation and team teaching
	Students composing on computers	Introduce and discuss alternative pedagogies
	Course of study evolving as result of student productivity and changing expectations of teachers	Train staff in use of tool software: spreadsheets, databases, graphics, hypermedia, communications
		Introduce video disc and scanner technology

Table 3.1 Support for instructional evolution in technology-rich classrooms (*continued*)

Phase	Expectation	Support
Appropriation	Increased focus on higher-order skills	Routinize peer observations and group discussions of events and consequences
	Experimentation with interdisciplinary, project-based instruction	Reexamine project mission and goals
	Experimentation with team teaching	Build awareness of alternative student assessment strategies, i.e., performance-based assessment and portfolio assessment strategies
	Experimentation with student grouping	
	Conflict with traditional schedules and assessment techniques	Encourage and support conference attendance and teacher presentations
	Experimentation with scheduling and assessment strategies	
Invention	Establishment of higher learning standards	Encourage collaboration between teachers and researchers
	Implementation of integrated curriculum	Encourage teachers to write about and publish their experiences
	Balanced and strategic use of direct teaching and project-based teaching	Explore telecommunications as way to keep teachers in contact with innovators outside of district
	Integration of alternative modes of student assessment	Create opportunities for teachers to mentor other teachers

write about and publish their experiences as innovators. The advent of the World Wide Web and numerous teacher bulletin boards and chat areas provides a perfect opportunity.

There are important caveats to the strategy of focusing on changing teachers' beliefs as a condition for instructional change. First, there are risks associated with making successful change efforts a matter of achieving a series of personal triumphs rather than recognizing the process as an organizational, systemic, or cultural phenomenon. Any teacher in the process of change is an actor surrounded by other actors and institutionalized principles. If there is no change in the larger system, the struggling teacher is doomed to frustration and the innovation to abandonment (Bowers, 1973; Schiffer, 1979). This condition led to Mrs. Bennett's resignation from the ACOT project, as described in Chapter 2. Second, beliefs are an inherently complex concept. Although plans for reform may appear rational, reformers must accept that beliefs, tied as they are to personal insights, significant personal moments, and to significant others, affect behavior in outwardly irrational ways. "There are no clear, logical rules for determining the relevance of beliefs to real world events and situations" (Nespor, 1987, p. 321). Third, groups bound by commitment to change, sharing reflections and shaping new beliefs, can lose their objectivity and create new problems (Dwyer, 1981; Hoffer, 1951; Janis, 1972; Smith & Dwyer, 1979).

In sum, instructional change can proceed only with a corresponding change in beliefs about instruction and learning. Teachers' beliefs can only be modified while teachers are in the thick of change—taking risks and facing uncertainty. Bringing significant change to the way we do schooling is a complex proposition fraught with setbacks. The experience of the ACOT project demonstrates the value of taking a long-term perspective on change and making the necessary personal and organizational commitments to bring about that change. To the observer, hoping for quick evidence of the efficacy of innovations, computers or otherwise, the process can only be frustrating and inconclusive. To those dedicated enough to make the commitment, the process can be very rewarding.

In describing teachers' experiences in the stages of instructional evolution, we touched briefly upon various issues of concern for teachers such as classroom management, student and teacher roles, student engagement, and teachers' relationships with one another. In the next four chapters, we examine those issues in greater depth, highlighting both the challenges and rewards of working in technology-rich classrooms.

4

Managing a
Technology-Rich
Classroom

If I had my druthers, I don't think I would ever look at a computer again. One of my students got into the network and lost lots of information because he doesn't know what he is doing. It's a typical situation, and it's caused a major problem because now the computers are down. There are so many variables like this that we deal with on a day-to-day basis that I didn't anticipate being part of this program. I'm anxious for the weekend so I don't have to do anything with computers.

Every teacher has an occasional bad day. But few teachers identify a student's experiments on a computer network as the source of their frustrations. Although David Mendez brought years of teaching experience to his job, the introduction of computers into his classroom significantly altered his teaching environment. In many ways, Mr. Mendez felt like a novice again. Neither he nor the other ACOT teachers completely anticipated the range of student misbehavior, changes in the physical environment, shifts in teachers' roles, and technical problems that would accompany new technology. Nor did they anticipate how quickly they would learn to utilize technology to their advantage in managing the classroom in areas such as grading, record keeping, individualizing instruction, and developing new materials. Whereas in the beginning of the project teachers sometimes thought only of how technology increased their workload, before long many teachers doubted they could ever return to a traditional classroom. This chapter describes how teachers moved from frustration to success in coping with changes brought about by the introduction of computers to their classrooms.

STAGES OF CONCERN

During the first three stages of instructional evolution (introduced in Chapter 3), teachers had to struggle with classroom management concerns. During the entry stage, teachers were preoccupied with their own adequacy. Their concerns centered on themselves and their ability to maintain control over the classroom and the students. In a completely new classroom environment, teachers spent a considerable amount of time reacting to problems instead of anticipating and avoiding them. In the adoption stage, teachers began not only to anticipate problems but to develop strategies for solving them. During the adaptation stage, teachers focused on the effects of their teaching on students and began to utilize technology to their advantage in managing the classroom. In the last two stages, appropriation and invention, teachers' management concerns abated as their instructional approaches and management strategies became intertwined. The following sections examine teachers' concerns during the first three stages of the evolutionary process, when the most significant changes related to classroom management occurred.

STAGE I: ENTRY

During the entry stage, project teachers frequently found themselves unable to anticipate problems in their technology-rich classrooms.

We discovered a common pattern of concerns that included the following categories: student misbehavior and attitudes, the physical environment, technical problems and software management, and the dynamics of the classroom environment.

Student Misbehavior and Attitudes

Although adding technology to the classroom initially had little effect on teachers' instructional behaviors, the introduction of computers to classrooms opened up a whole new realm of student misbehavior. As students learned to use disks and software, some also discovered how to illegally copy software, how to protect their disks from teacher access, and how to sabotage other students' work. In the words of one teacher, the computers provided "a real opportunity for the freshmen to irritate the sophomores." Seemingly innocent classroom activities became an opportunity for student misconduct. For instance, during a telecommunications activity with a class at another school, students began exchanging insults. With the interactive technology, the teacher had no opportunity to preview, and censor if necessary, the students' messages. In classrooms hooked to online services, teachers also worried that students could gain access to inappropriate or objectionable materials.

New methods for cheating also accompanied the new technology. Knowing that the teacher could no longer rely on handwriting to distinguish an individual student's work, some students simply stole other people's disks and tried to relabel them for themselves. Another common tactic involved taking someone's disk, copying work, and returning the disk to its original spot. One teacher explains the simple process:

> I discovered that students had copied each other's data without the students knowing it—by using the disk before class. The computer makes it much easier to cheat. In 5 to 10 seconds, a student can copy work and not even know what it said.

Other students, described by teachers as "computer wizards," used more advanced techniques for cheating. For example, as the following quote describes, one student figured out how to get 100% on the computerized algebra test without working through any of the steps on his scratch paper.

> When he held up his hand to say he was through after 20 minutes, I went over to check, but he had done nothing on the

scratch paper . . . I had him go over the problems with me to show how he would do them, but he could really do only about 20 out of the 60 or 70 [problems] on the test . . . Somehow Jim figured out how to get the 100% in the computer without doing the work to earn it.

In many cases of student misbehavior, the actions stemmed from children's inquisitive nature. For instance, teachers found out that students had been taking apart the mice to see how they work. However, in putting them back together, parts would invariably end up missing. Other students experimented with magnets to see if "they really do erase a disk." "They did," reported a disgruntled teacher. Some students discovered how to read the telecommunications files of teachers, and in one classroom a student told the rest of the class how to get into the teacher's management system. While teachers admired the students' curiosity, they decried the results of these misguided adventures. One of the most frustrating situations for teachers occurred when students, intentionally or unintentionally, caused problems with the computer network system. Network damage affected the entire class, disrupting the instructional activities. Frequently, a network problem shut down all of the computers in the classroom.

Teachers also found themselves unable, in the beginning, to predict student attitudes about working with the computers. Some students became so enamored with technology that they became unwilling to do work with paper and pencil when their classroom or home computers were broken. Several of the software programs intrigued students to the point that they openly resisted when teachers decided to move on to other activities. As one teacher analyzed the problem, the difficulty stemmed from "trying to fit open-ended software into a time-structured environment." In addition, some teachers felt that the availability of software at individual workstations allowed students "too much control" over what they elected to do. Often the tempting software and the allure of the computers made it difficult for students to concentrate on other types of classroom activities. As one teacher put it:

Study time is a problem time. Students think that just because that computer is sitting there, they have to have their hot little hands on those keyboards . . . They just get on the computer and anything they can call up they have to have their hands on it.

Another teacher pointed out:

> I've found that when the computers are on, the students not
> using them have a very difficult time maintaining their
> concentration on whatever else they're doing, even if their
> backs are to the computers.

The computers became not only a source of distraction for the
students but also physical shields to hide occasional off-task behavior
when doing noncomputer activities. Even high school students could
"hide behind their computers" to avoid working on the assigned task.
In addition, the use of home computers provided some students a
host of new excuses for not completing their homework. One teacher
complained:

> We really should be keeping a log of all the excuses that are given
> for not doing bulletin-board homework. Students are the same: it
> does not matter if they are doing their homework by candlelight
> or telecommunications, only the tools and technology change.
> Excuses remain. Here are the three best ones for this week: "My
> telephone cord is too short." "Momma gave my adapter away."
> "My modem messed up and erased all my messages."

Hardware problems on the home computer became the most typical
excuse. One teacher, after finally catching on to the scheme, started
keeping a record of all the excuses given by the students.

The Physical Environment

The addition of computers to the classroom also created a number of
problems related to the physical environment. For instance, the
classroom lighting and the glare from the windows hindered the students' ability to produce digitized pictures and to use the liquid display panel for presentations. Chalk dust, a common element in most
classrooms, gathered in the keyboards and computers, resulting in
problems. Power outages caused major disruptions in classroom
activities, and sometimes students experienced unexplained electrical
interference on the computer monitors.

Extremes in the weather played havoc with classroom computers. Hot weather caused computers to crash in schools without air
conditioning, and fans did little to alleviate the problem. Powerful

rainstorms flooded several classrooms, damaging some equipment and making it dangerous to turn on the computers. At one school, the weather created a static electricity problem:

> We had an exceptionally bad time with static electricity . . . I am concerned that we are going to lose some disks; we have already lost one. I've really talked to the kids about grounding themselves before they touch anything, and I hope it sinks through.

Teachers also expressed surprise and frustration at the extra time spent setting up and arranging equipment. Besides the initial setup of the classroom, teachers found themselves dismantling the computers so that they could repair the tables, rearranging the equipment for special projects, setting up new desks, and disassembling and reassembling classrooms because of changes in room assignments. To their dismay, teachers who had become accustomed to neat and orderly classrooms now found them cluttered and crowded with the addition of computers, printers, cables, disks, papers, and other related paraphernalia. They needed to provide individual attention to students as they worked on their computers, but they found it increasingly difficult to move around the room. As one teacher phrased it, "I am constantly tripping over technology of some sort; the room is just not big enough to hold everything that we need for it." Given these additional demands, teachers became particularly annoyed when other groups, such as community-service and senior-citizen classes, used their classrooms and left them in disarray.

The changing physical environment of the classroom also made it more challenging to organize various instructional groupings. Several teachers expressed frustration when trying to arrange coherent group work with computers. They could no longer simply rearrange some chairs and desks or tables into group settings.

Technical Problems and Software Management

ACOT teachers encountered numerous technical problems because of the amount of equipment they dealt with every day. Technical problems upset both their daily and long-range plans and, over the years, were the source of most of their complaints.

Another inconvenience ACOT teachers dealt with was having computers out for repair. Despite the teachers' sense of urgency, repairs typically took a period of weeks. Teachers also experienced problems with printers. Since the students did most of their assignments on the computers, they had a large volume of work that needed to be printed. The heavy use of printers and the variety of people using them seemed to contribute to the frequent malfunctioning and breakdown of that equipment. Teachers noted that printers frequently jammed, increasing the time needed to get student assignments printed. Also, the number of printers didn't always match the demand, they said, creating a bottleneck. In the words of one teacher:

> Printers have been jamming up, there are fewer of them in the room, and they require constant attention to get assignments printed. It took 20 minutes for one group of 30 students this week.

When numerous students tried to print at the same time, a backlog of printing jobs resulted. However, when many students in the class simultaneously tried to log on or save onto the computer network, a new problem emerged: a network jam or breakdown. In one of the classrooms, the problem occurred more frequently on one side of the room than the other because of the uneven distribution of computers. Network problems were serious for teachers because they rarely had the expertise to fix the problem themselves and because their lesson plans were totally disrupted.

Introducing computers into the classrooms also meant that teachers had to deal with new instructional tools and their accompanying bugs, which could cause them to malfunction. Sometimes software programs would lock up (stop responding to commands) because of an error. One of the most frustrating problems resulted from incompatibility between software and computers or printers:

> The assignment ran all right on the new printers, but the older printers caused problems. Some students could complete the work and some could not. It was really frustrating and not a happy sight, to say the least.

Beyond the technical problems, teachers encountered a variety of management concerns related to software and disks. Software frequently arrived late, and copyright restrictions made it difficult to acquire enough classroom copies for student use. As one teacher related, "This year we have a new spelling series which has software that coordinates with each lesson. Unfortunately, the software is copyprotected; we have not been able to reach the salesman."

In one case, schools purchased software that didn't meet the advertised claims, and the company responded by telling teachers to wait for a new release. At several locations, local suppliers were unable to keep enough disks in stock to meet the demands of the ACOT classrooms. Some teachers became overwhelmed by the sheer number of disks and programs with which they had to work. One teacher pointed out, "One of the things which slows us down is the constant booting of disks and the constant need to find which one of 500 floppies has the information I want. That is a real chore."

Dynamics of the Classroom Environment

Another concern of the first stage centered on teachers' abilities to understand the dynamics of the classroom environment. Many teachers were initially troubled by the noise of printers and keyboards, and of students moving freely around the classroom. One commented, "Sometimes the screech of the printers is absolutely maddening in the classroom. I can't do anything until the printers are off." Another teacher found that "there is a great deal of freedom in the way the work is set up, which leads to a lot of noise and talking."

Having become accustomed to the structure of students sitting in their seats and the teacher up in front of the classroom, some teachers worried whether students were on task and learning (see Chapter 5). For instance, a teacher wondered if students "are really on task with the teachers just moving around the room. I am also concerned about whether the students can really learn without me up front in charge. It takes getting used to." Another teacher pointed out that "it is hard to allow the kids the freedom they need to move about the room for individual and group work."

During the entry stage, teachers felt unprepared to deal with unanticipated management problems and focused their energies on managing the classroom rather than becoming instructionally innovative. As teachers moved into the second stage, adoption, the intensity of their concerns with management decreased.

STAGE 2: ADOPTION

In the adoption stage, teachers began not only to anticipate problems but also to develop strategies for solving them. When problems occurred, teachers were now able to make necessary changes.

To deal with student misbehavior, teachers developed strategies aimed at the specific problems. Since the technology was both a prime attraction of students and a source of misbehavior, many teachers started to place restrictions on its use. In most cases, individual students lost their computer privileges for a period of time, but sometimes teachers imposed group restrictions. For example, one teacher decided to "not have the computers on before school, during lunch, or for study hall at the end of the day as a punishment for illegal copying."

Teachers also became aware of the variety of cheating schemes in progress and adopted strategies—such as confronting each student individually, holding class discussions on ethics, and imposing grading penalties. Some teachers became as ingenious in devising solutions as students had been in finding ways to cheat. These teachers figured out how to use technology to catch the culprits and stifle recurrences. For example, a high school class had been given an insect-collection-and-database assignment, and a number of students appeared to have copied data from one disk to another. The teacher described how he solved the problem:

> Technology comes to the rescue of the teacher by allowing the teacher to become aware of the "sharing." When I merged all the students' databases into one massive database, I was able to sort on various fields. For example, by sorting on the "Common Name" field, it became apparent that several students found 17-year cicadas on August 22 at Rocky Fork Country Club at 12:00 p.m. The insect is lying on the ground in a forest—sleeping. It's like playing the game "What's wrong with this picture?" Cicadas are tree insects (not ground), and don't sleep in the daytime. It also makes one wonder how all those students happened to be at a country club in another part of town all at the same time. The students quickly admitted the error of their ways when I showed the merged database to them.

Technology also came to the aid of a teacher searching for a way to keep his curious students from finding the built-in answers to his computerized tests. Since some of his students delighted in the challenge of discovering the solution keys, he scrambled to learn more and more about the software. Eventually, the teacher came up with a strategy—assigning a global variable to the scoring portion of the test—that he felt confident would keep students from cheating.

In dealing with problems related to the physical environment, teachers encountered more limited solutions. In some cases, the ACOT classes could be moved to more spacious classrooms, but more frequently, they could do little about the size of the classroom itself. Consequently, teachers arranged classrooms to allow for the greatest amount of free space, and they developed systems for organizing and storing disks, printer paper, software, and other computer items. For some problems, teachers requested changes in the physical features of their classrooms. For example, teachers asked for glareproof windows and static-free carpeting. Whiteboards replaced chalkboards in the classrooms, to reduce the amount of chalk dust.

To counteract the amount of time spent setting up and arranging equipment, some teachers started to enlist student help in setting up computers and furniture. At one site the coordinator scheduled a full week of planning time before school started to set up the rooms. In her words, "We really feel we're off to a smooth start this year. We took a week of planning time before school began to get ready, and that really helped."

Technical problems continued to plague teachers over the years. Although some sites and some teachers successfully reduced the number of technical problems, no one completely eliminated them. Given the number of computers and the frequency of use, technical problems became a fact of life in the classrooms. The most ideal solution for dealing with technical problems occurred at a site that employed an on-site computer technician:

> So far on the home scene, we have had one monitor (in its third year of use) go bad. At school, we either don't have very many problems, or we don't notice them. Our technician has most repairs done in a half-hour, so the down time isn't long enough to become irritating.

However, not all of the sites could afford such a luxury. Consequently, most teachers developed alternative lesson plans to use when computers were down. With experience and increased knowledge of computers and software, teachers and coordinators gradually became more adept at avoiding problems and, when problems did occur, narrowing down the source of the difficulty. One teacher, after completing computer-repair training, was delighted to discover that he could solve problems that puzzled even the district technician. He reported, "Last week I was in Chicago for service training . . . I am already seeing some of the benefits from the trip. I have already solved a problem that the district technician could not solve."

To deal with jamming of printers, the noise level, and loss of class time for printing, many teachers adopted rules for use of printers, restricting who could operate them and when. Several teachers had students save their work onto one data disk and then printed it at the end of the day. In some classrooms, teachers secured additional printers to alleviate the backlog of printing jobs and continued to have students do their own printing.

Securing additional equipment was the obvious solution to many teachers' complaints about lack of equipment. As they received additional equipment, teachers reported favorable improvements in their classroom environments. However, as one teacher pointed out, increases in equipment brought increases in expectations:

> If we go way back, I wanted one computer for my class, then when I got one I wanted two and then 15 and so on. Well, now we have one laser [disc] player and one scanner, and already the kids are standing in line to use them. We have one 20-megabyte hard drive, and it is filled up and no longer useful. We need a bigger storage unit . . . It just seems that what you've got is never enough.

As teachers became accustomed to new technology, they gradually adjusted to changes in the classroom environment. By increasing their knowledge, they enhanced their abilities to manage these technology-rich classrooms. One teacher regularly attended a computer applications class taught by a colleague in the school, and another teacher began an individual study program to learn how to type correctly. Many teachers spent their summers becoming more familiar with software already being used by the students and previewing new software. Through the process of preparing for and teaching their classes, teachers learned new techniques and applications that enhanced their instruction the following year. As one teacher described:

> I'm feeling really good about the things I've found out this year for ways to use the computer in instruction, and I'm looking forward to working it in as I make my lesson plans this summer. I can take an introductory idea and expand it.

Just as increased knowledge aided teachers, substitutes and parents benefited from learning more about using computers. By holding parent meetings, teachers could help parents feel more comfortable about supervising their children's homework on the computer. Similarly, substitutes who participated in computer training workshops became capable and eager replacements in ACOT classrooms. For example, one teacher found that

> The substitute teachers were not only unafraid to [work with the students and the computers], some of them requested that they be given the opportunity to do so. I was a little surprised, but very pleased! We have frequently invited the subs to participate in workshops, and it seems to have paid off.

Increased teacher knowledge also had a noticeable impact on student engagement (see Chapter 6), lessening discipline problems that had plagued teachers during the beginning of the project. For instance, one elementary teacher discussed her surprise at how well she was able to conduct a lesson during her second year with the project:

> Today being on task was not a problem . . . I was absolutely amazed at how easy [the writing program] was for the children . . . The kids' eyes were just glued to the computer screen . . . Last year, I wasn't that familiar with the software and wasn't positive what the next screen would be. This year, I could teach it confidently.

The addition of technology to classrooms eventually led to different instructional goals for many teachers. They viewed instruction in terms of larger goals and worried less about whether they were teaching specific content to students. As one teacher summarized:

> I think that if you're going to make use of technology, you have to let go of having to cover specific material, from a specific book, by a certain time. I'd like to be free of these constraints. I have some proposals for next year.

Some features of the new classroom environment, which troubled teachers initially, became less important to them. They began to accept the necessity for students to move freely around the classroom and became less bothered by the noise level. One teacher went so far as to say, "I love to hear the sound of the computer keys as they [the students] work. ACOT classrooms do have different sounds, don't they?"

Initially overwhelmed by unexpected problems brought about by the introduction of technology into their classrooms, teachers in the adoption stage quickly rebounded and became adept at problem solving. Although problems with hardware and software never completely disappeared, teachers began to take pride in their skills at troubleshooting and repairing equipment, in their knowledge about technology, and in their abilities to change plans when last-minute problems arose. In the next stage, adaptation, teachers capitalized on these skills and designed strategies to lessen their workloads.

STAGE 3: ADAPTATION

In the adaptation stage, teachers used the technology to their advantage in managing the classroom. Rather than just troubleshooting, teachers developed techniques for monitoring student work, keeping records, grading tests, developing new materials, and individualizing instruction. In learning more about computers and software, they discovered that technology could save them time rather than create additional demands. One teacher expressed the change in teachers' perspectives this way:

> I came into the program with a negative attitude about technology complicating things and being more of a hassle than it is worth. Even today when my disk failed and I spent a half-hour saving the data, I have come around to the idea that technology intelligently used can simplify one's life and free up time and energy for other things.

One of the first areas where teachers learned to use technology to their advantage was record keeping. By creating databases and spreadsheets on the computer, they significantly decreased the amount of time spent keeping track of everything from teaching materials to grades. After teachers started using databases, they uncovered more ways to use this tool. As one teacher reflected on his conversation with a colleague:

> I mentioned to Martha yesterday how much I love databases. It seems like a silly thing to say to somebody, but I do. I didn't realize when I was department chair that when I was doing organizational work, I was creating databases. I was always drawing little grids or charts to keep track of things. I didn't do it as much as I would have because they were so laborious to create. But now I create them for everything.

In one classroom, students created a database that included all of the software they had heard about or used. In about 20 minutes, students had created the database and rated the software. The teacher envisioned that the database would help teachers evaluate future software purchases. Another teacher, who previously had created spreadsheets that calculated the amount of money each child brought in from the fundraising campaign, decided to develop spreadsheets for students to use in keeping track of their scores on assignments. She commented, "The spreadsheet automatically calculates their percentage correct and sets a marker if their percentage is below 80%. Students then have to complete as many more problems as they need to in order to reach 80%." In addition to using spreadsheets for their master records, teachers created modified versions that students could access to verify their progress. This eliminated the need for students to question the teacher individually.

Computers also proved to be a great boon when it came time for teachers to calculate grades. Some teachers used commercial grading programs, while others developed their own. In both cases, the time needed to compute and record grades was greatly reduced. As one teacher commented:

> Figuring out grades for my 60 students was much different than in the past . . . It took me only 30 minutes instead of six hours or more. This program allowed me to juggle with the weighting of the grades . . . I now post grades every Friday because it's so easy to do the grades.

Another related:

> I only had to go around the room and enter the test grades into my spreadsheet to average the whole year's grades. That really saved time, and the whole year's grades are done.

For the special education teachers, one of the most time-consuming tasks was preparing required IEP's (Individual Education Plans) for each student. After some trial and error with different formats, one site developed a workable form that could be used by special education teachers to simplify the process. A teacher described the change in preparing the plans:

> We have been busy preparing for the IEP conferences . . . It has been another new adventure for us since we have never used

computerized IEP forms to show parents and ourselves where
the students are and the areas they need to work on . . . Once I
figured out a way to evaluate the students in language, I began
feeling very positive toward the whole process . . . Since we are
using the computer program . . . writing the IEPs is not the chore
I used to hear the special education teachers complaining about.
Hurray for High Tech!!!!

As teachers shared their ideas with one another and experimented with the computers, they came up with improved techniques
for developing assignments and tests. For example, teachers could
type assignments directly into the network rather than running off
separate assignment sheets:

In physical science, Steve is downloading his templates on
chemical reactions he developed last year . . . the students have
access to the total assignment on the network and are working
through it much more quickly and with more understanding.
Many of them never used paper and pencil on the assignment at
all. They download Steve's handouts to their computers, work on
the tasks assigned, and send the final copy of their work to the
printer to be picked up by Steve. No more pages and pages of
handouts that are lost, replaced, and lost again.

The computer also made it easier for teachers to discourage cheating
by making three or four different forms of a test.

But one of the main advantages was immediate feedback for students on both tests and assignments. As one teacher reported,
"Recently I gave a science test and students were able to get results
within 15 minutes of completion . . . There's nothing like immediate
feedback, not to mention the amount of time saved." Another teacher
came up with a format that used immediate feedback to help students "discover" mathematical concepts. For instance, in an algebra
lesson on factoring trinomials, students were asked to put in values
for the designated variables. The computer responded with either
a "not valid" or "this is it" message. The purpose of guessing the
values was to help students understand the significance of the middle
term. The teacher reported, "The students were catching on to the
fact through trial and error that the middle term was really important in coming up with the correct factors. That sometimes slips by
them when each student does not have the opportunity to have
immediate feedback."

Besides providing immediate feedback to students, technology allowed teachers to update their tests and materials on a frequent basis. For example, one teacher used the morning newspaper to create current-events assignments for her classes that day:

> I can put together a newspaper assignment for my first period very quickly. Twenty minutes before class, I skim the newspaper and make up assignments that are pertinent to today's news. It's really no great effort with the computer.

Computers also enabled teachers to individualize instruction in many subject areas. Students could work through material at their own pace because the technology made it possible for teachers to manage the range of instruction. As one teacher described:

> The individualized math program has been my greatest success this year. My children are doing so well in math and are doing it at their own level . . . We've been using the software as a backup for each of the objectives. I feel really good about the math.

In addition, the computer facilitated reteaching and retesting of certain students because it could generate both tests and study guides.

As teachers became more familiar with computer applications and software, they developed strategies for increasing the amount of material they could cover during the school day. For instance, math teachers reported that they had been able to cut back on school time spent on arithmetic skills, relying more on computer homework for arithmetic and spending school time on problem solving. A science teacher who formerly spent 10 complete class periods on a biology lesson about DNA modeling used the drawing feature of the computer to design a similar lesson that required only 40 minutes of class time. An elementary teacher commented how letter writing was so much easier to teach on the computer because of the editing feature. With less time being spent on basic topics, teachers could enhance and improve their curriculum. For instance, one teacher said, "Academically, I have to add things to the curriculum to make it more challenging. The computer is a tremendous help in this area."

As teachers' abilities to use technology to their advantage increased, their attitudes changed too. Whereas earlier they worried about classrooms becoming technology centered rather than in-

struction centered, they now described the classrooms as more
learner centered:

> The setup in ACOT makes it possible for the classroom to be
> more learner centered than teacher centered. I find myself being
> more of a facilitator. I am sure that I will change even more as I
> learn new techniques.

Teachers no longer viewed the process of learning to use the computers as infringing on the curriculum. Instead, they described the technology as support for the curriculum. One teacher, who developed
techniques for using laser video discs and animation in his biology
materials, suggested that "the content is the same, but how we
deliver it is completely different."

This difference in the delivery of the content translated into
increased student interest and attention. Teachers now were able to
use the technology to enhance student motivation and interest while
decreasing the number of discipline problems. Students spent more
time on task and even asked for additional work on the computer
(see Chapter 6). The increased student motivation extended beyond
the classroom. A ninth-grade student surprised her teacher by sharing a tip that she had read in a computer magazine the night before:

> When the printer is first ready, it prints a warm-up sheet. One of
> our ninth graders came over and told me, "If you pull the paper
> tray out just a little before you turn on the printer, you can save
> the sheet of paper. I read that tip last night."

Besides increased interest, students exhibited more pride in their
work. With the graphics capabilities and the printer, the students
enjoyed producing assignments that "look so good." As teachers
became less threatened by some students' exceptional abilities on the
computer, they reframed their views about teacher role and used
these students as peer teachers. This made it possible to provide
more individual help to students who were experiencing difficulties.
In addition, the teachers themselves drew upon these students' expertise when problems occurred (see Chapter 5).

As teachers learned how to use technology to their advantage in
managing the classroom, they discovered that their attitudes about
computers changed. In contrast to the beginning of the project, when
teachers expressed concerns about their "computerized classrooms,"

they now worried about having to teach in classrooms without access to technology. As one person commented, "That computer has become so much a part of my body that I just don't seem to be able to work without it." Another stated:

> The power was not working in our classroom, and we had no computers. But the class had to go on. We had to go back to the good old days of pencil and paper. It was so strange not hearing the computer go on and not hearing the keypads going . . . I had the feeling I was in a different classroom, and I didn't like that classroom.

CLASSROOM MANAGEMENT REVISITED

Classroom management is not a skill that can be mastered once and for all. Changes in the classroom environment can significantly alter the success of a teacher's tried-and-true management principles. The ACOT teachers, though primarily veterans, discovered that managing a technology-rich classroom was significantly different from many of their previous experiences. After struggling with unanticipated management concerns, they eventually came to use technology in both classroom management and instruction.

Initially, project teachers felt much like beginning teachers who identify classroom discipline as their primary problem area (Veenman, 1984). Overwhelmed by their inability to anticipate problems, they often were unable to make necessary changes when difficulties did occur. With experience, however, they began not only to anticipate problems but to develop strategies for solving and avoiding them. The most significant changes in instruction occurred after teachers resolved many concerns related to the use of technology. By this point teachers focused on the effects of their teaching on students and began to utilize technology to their advantage in managing the classroom. They used technology to enhance student motivation, interest, and learning, as well as to decrease discipline problems. They incorporated the technology into their teaching in such a way that they couldn't imagine teaching without it. Teaching in a technology-rich classroom had become a beneficial way of life.

ACOT teachers' struggles and triumphs in managing technology-rich environments highlight four issues related to classroom practice: the influence of context on classroom management, the link between management and instruction, the role of teacher education, and the value of technological resources for teacher productivity. These are described next.

The Influence of Context on Classroom Management

As the classroom context changes, so do management concerns. Intrinsic features of the classroom context create constant pressures that shape the task of teaching (Doyle, 1980). In technology-rich classrooms at least four of these features have an even greater influence on teaching: multidimensionality, simultaneity, immediacy, and unpredictability. Multidimensionality refers to the large quantity of events and tasks in classrooms. With the addition of technology and a shift to constructivist teaching, the number of events and tasks increases almost exponentially. As demonstrated in the ACOT classrooms, the sheer amount of equipment and supplies disrupted the previous organizational arrangements. The number of concurrent events in the classroom, called simultaneity, also increases significantly as students work individually or in small groups on computers. Moreover, students often are working on different tasks, requiring the teacher to monitor numerous activities at once.

The pace of classroom events, referred to as immediacy, often becomes even more rapid in technology-rich classrooms, requiring immediate action on the part of the teachers. However, the intrinsic feature that most alters teaching when using technology is unpredictability. In all classrooms, events often take unexpected directions and interruptions are frequent, making it difficult "to anticipate how an activity will go on a particular day with a particular group of students" (Doyle, 1986, p. 395). The changes in the classroom environment brought about by the addition of technology lead to an even higher level of unpredictability. For instance, as early as the second year of the ACOT project, most teachers learned to expect occasional technological problems and planned accordingly. Yet, when new software, new hardware, or new students arrived on the scene, many teachers found themselves temporarily back in the entry stage, facing unanticipated concerns.

The Link Between Management and Instruction

ACOT teachers' experiences illustrate the importance of linking management approaches and instructional strategies. Management is commonly viewed as a prerequisite to instruction and as something to get out of the way so that teaching can occur (Doyle, 1986). In practice, however, classroom management and instruction are closely intertwined, in that a minimal level of orderliness is needed for instruction to occur. Conversely, teachers find that meaningful and engaging instructional activities capture and sustain student attention, thus decreasing behavior problems.

Classroom management has been identified as the most important factor influencing student learning (Wang, Haertel, & Walberg, 1993). Without management skills, the absence or presence of technology has little discernible impact on classroom instruction. Teachers unable to manage and organize a technology-rich classroom will struggle for survival simply because they cannot keep students involved in the learning process. On the other hand, teachers may be able to organize a classroom with technology but not provide meaningful learning opportunities for students.

Over time, the ACOT teachers used technology to their advantage in both enhancing student learning and managing the classroom. As they adopted a more constructivist approach, they described their classrooms as student centered rather than technology centered or instruction centered. Changes in instructional strategies similarly led to management systems more aligned with constructivism. In classrooms aimed at promoting problem solving and meaningful learning, their classroom management approaches needed to elicit more than obedience, quiet, and order. Research indicates that to implement a curriculum that seeks to foster self-motivated, active learners, teachers also must employ a management system that increasingly allows students to operate as self-regulated and risk-taking learners (McCaslin & Good, 1992).

The Importance of Teacher Education in Classroom Management

The strong link in practice between management and instruction warrants a similar connection in preparing teachers to use technology. However, in teacher education, classroom management and technology are typically treated as separate and distinct subjects. For instance, in the *Handbook of Research on Teacher Education* (Sikula, 1996), the chapter on classroom management includes nothing about technology, and the chapter on technology and teacher education makes no mention of classroom management.

Classroom management is a common theme of in-service training for teachers and is included in virtually all teacher preparation programs, most often as a topic within methods or curriculum courses (Jones, 1996). A 10-member panel on the preparation of beginning teachers listed knowledge of how to manage a classroom, along with knowledge of subject matter and understanding of students' sociological background, as the major areas of expertise needed by beginning teachers (Boyer, 1984). Technology doesn't yet command a similar status in teacher education. The universal conclusion of the literature on technology and teacher education is that teacher education, particularly preservice, is not preparing educators to work in technology-enriched classrooms (Willis & Mehlinger, 1996). Some reports suggest that the vast majority of teachers have had little or no training related to using computers in their teaching (Office of Technology Assessment, 1988). An additional concern is that training focuses on hardware and software rather than on the connection between computers and the curriculum (Bork, 1991; Knupfer, 1991).

The experiences of the ACOT teachers suggest that both management and instructional issues need to be included in teacher education efforts related to technology. Many of the management struggles that teachers encountered could be averted with appropriate preparation and support. The critical component is not a set of specific management strategies for technology-rich classrooms but rather an understanding of the context. When classroom management information is related to the context in which teachers will be working, they can then link issues of content, instruction, and management (Brophy, 1988).

The Value of Technological Sources for Teacher Productivity

Finally, technology offers valuable resources for teachers in carrying out many aspects of their jobs. The Office of Technology Assessment (1995) reports that teachers often see the value of students using technology but are less aware of the resources technology can offer them as professionals in fulfilling their responsibilities. Similarly, the ACOT teachers initially focused on technology as a tool for student learning and had to deal with increased workload and drawbacks associated with implementation. They later discovered how technology could increase their productivity in tasks such as grading, keeping records, developing materials, monitoring student work, and individualizing instruction. Their initial fears and concerns about technology increasing their workloads gave way to confidence and a reliance on technology. When teachers recognize that the use of technology stands to benefit both them and their students, they will more willingly invest the extra time and effort needed to integrate technology into the classroom. The next chapter describes how the use of technology led to beneficial changes in teacher and student roles.

5

Redefining
Student and Teacher
Roles

❝ First year of project: *I lectured no more than 10 minutes in science today. For the rest of the period the kids worked on a project. What effect will this have on their learning?*

Two years later: *As the kids are presenting their computer projects, I'm able to allow them to assume the role of teacher and I assume the role of a student . . . Sometimes we ask for others in the class to volunteer the information first. I kind of become the final person that can give information rather than the initial person in class.*

The following year: *I think the kids are gaining an extraordinary amount of . . . knowledge . . . even though they're doing it on their own and it's not being fed to them by a teacher standing in front.* ❞   — John Erickson's Log

The above excerpts trace the development of a veteran high school science teacher involved in the ACOT project. In the first entry, Mr. Erickson is concerned because he does not spend the entire class period in his traditional way—imparting knowledge to his students. In contrast, three years later he is convinced that abandoning the "sage on the stage" model of teaching will lead to extraordinary learning.

This chapter examines the role shifts that occurred for both teachers and students as they struggled to adopt and use the technology. As was the case with Mr. Erickson, the use of the lecture–recitation–seat work model decreased and there was greater emphasis on students working together—two features that characterize constructivist classrooms. In this chapter, we discuss how and why teachers began to use student expertise in the classroom, describe how the roles of student experts expanded as teachers recognized the benefits of student interaction and collaboration, and offer several issues to consider in redefining classroom roles.

USING STUDENT EXPERTS IN THE CLASSROOM

At the outset of the project, teachers, like their students, faced learning how to use a multitude of technology. As experienced teachers—knowledgeable about the curriculum, classroom management, and principles of learning—some teachers felt discomfort about knowing little more than their students about the technology. In fact, before too long, some of their students had become experts in using particular computer applications, software, or hardware, and knew more than both their teachers and their peers.

Peer Tutoring

At all of the sites, students began helping their peers and their teachers by providing technical assistance and tutoring on the use of the new technology. At first, students' role as "teacher" was sporadic, spontaneous, and unstructured. Rather than sitting quietly and waiting for their teacher to help them with the technology, students began to take the initiative and ask each other for assistance or volunteer information to one another. Even first-graders offered to teach their friends how to boot a disk or maneuver a mouse. This sudden increase in peer interaction disturbed teachers, such as Mrs. Bennett (see Chapter 2), who were accustomed to children raising their hands for permission to speak or leave their seats. Others, however, expressed delight about students' eagerness to share their knowledge:

> I was really pleased today with how the children finished their stories . . . One child using a drawing program didn't have enough room, and another child came over and showed him how to delete so he could have more room on his disk. I often wonder when the children discover and where they learn how to figure out the various pieces of software and the computer. I may have taught one—or none, and they have discovered on their own.

During the early stages of the project, the students rather than the teachers usually initiated peer tutoring. Frequently, teachers observed that if they taught one or two students how to do something on the computer, the rest of the class would not need teacher-directed instruction because they learned informally from their peers. Eventually teachers began to capitalize more formally on students' technological expertise rather than relying on the classroom grapevine. For example, some teachers assigned various software packages to different students, asking each student to become an expert with one particular software title or tool. Other teachers asked students to take software home to evaluate, as in this instance featuring Carl, a tenth-grader:

> Since Carl is already expert with one desktop publishing program, he is studying a competing product and coming up with a comparison on which product does what and which he would recommend if a school could only buy one. That should be valuable information for all of us.

Certain students began to play specialized roles in the classroom. For example, Mr. Erickson created his science tests on the computer with a hypermedia application. He quickly realized that Sam, one of his students, had a lot to teach him:

> Sam came in after class . . . and told me about all the things the kids could do to their test, if they really knew the hypermedia application, to enhance their grade . . . He showed me how to beat the test. From him, I picked up one to two things that I knew how to do, but hadn't done . . . It was a humbling experience.

After this experience, Mr. Erickson regularly counted on Sam's expertise when creating tests on the computer. For Mr. Erickson, Sam provided the "acid test" of whether or not his computerized test was well designed.

In the beginning of the project, teachers allowed their more capable students to serve formally as peer tutors, the assumption being that these high achievers would naturally excel in using the technology.

> One student got straight A's . . . Frieda has plans to use the computer to put together a newsletter to send home to parents. This particular student can then help teach the other kids to use the computer to design the newsletter.

Typically, teachers had their best students serve as peer tutors to save themselves time and to provide additional assistance to slower students. For instance, one teacher reported, "I am having the kids do a lot of work on the software manuals which I intend to use. They learn how to do the software programs while saving me prep time." Another teacher commented:

> Today I had one student who is really far ahead take a group of other students who had failed . . . and teach them. She did a good job and felt proud of herself, so I'm going to try it more often.

Gradually, however, most teachers realized that even less advanced students had much to offer their peers:

> During book editing time, Shelly finished her book and just very naturally went over and started helping Tom. He had messed up part of his book. She just went over to help and did a nice job. She's very limited herself, but it is interesting how limited some of these kids are and yet how they collaborate with others on projects. They do it very naturally and do a nice job on it.

Students' Attitudes About Classroom Roles

As teachers changed their views about teaching and learning, students also had to adjust their thinking about their roles in the classroom. New students, for example, were not accustomed to being able to ask their peers for assistance, since, in many classrooms, such interaction would be discouraged or even considered tantamount to cheating:

> We teachers and the experienced students have been trying to give the new students lots of help and support. Being able to ask classmates for help is strange to the newcomers.

After years of viewing the teacher as the classroom expert, some students also found it difficult to think of their peers as valuable sources of information:

> The tenth- and eleventh-graders are used to using each other as resources, asking questions and giving help, but it is new to the ninth-graders. It was really neat today to see them begin to work with each other, realizing that the teachers aren't their only source of help and support.

Eventually, however, students' beliefs about instruction shifted, and as they moved into the role of teacher, they started to see the benefits of particular instructional strategies. For example, in evaluating their peers' class presentations, students started to prefer methods requiring active involvement rather than passive forms of instruction such as the traditional lecture. As one teacher described:

> Most of the students taught the way I probably teach now—too much talking. I asked the students to reflect on how effective the groups were, and the students said, "Too much talking," when the students were just lecturing to the group. More and more we see that the active involvement is what grabs them. That's when they learn something.

As students gained more responsibility for their learning, they developed a greater sense of ownership in the process of instruction. They began to request additional opportunities to share with each other, and when teachers reverted to old instructional patterns, students quickly complained:

> The students love to share what they're learning on the computer. We decided to have a sharing meeting once a week . . . They really feel that the meetings belong to them and they're anxious to share. I tried to teach some things during one meeting and

they let me know that they were unhappy about me taking up their sharing time.

Unanticipated Benefits

While many teachers at first questioned the value of using students as teachers and wondered how it would affect learning, teachers soon realized that the benefits of this role shift went far beyond saving them time. Teachers saw less advanced students blossom, unpopular students gain peer approval, and unmotivated students stay in to work at recess:

> Joe is the talkative, annoying, misfit kind of kid which every teacher has had at some time. He loves the computer. He has not been popular with his peers, but he has caught on very quickly to the programming language. Other students are asking, "Can Joe come over and help me?" It is interesting to see how becoming an expert has influenced his class relationships.

In some cases, particular computer projects sparked these students' interest and tapped a hidden skill. For example, two high school students "who are noted as low achievers by everyone, including the students" got turned on by a robotics project and "worked seriously all the time." Some fourth-grade students "who do not usually receive as much recognition as others have proven to be very good at solving problems when staging original stories as a play using the software program." A first-grade student "who is low to average on academics is a whiz at word processing and finished all 21 lessons of that program today." In a fourth-grade classroom, a student "who doesn't do well in many courses is a whiz at patterns, and he was the only one to figure out the puzzle."

As teachers viewed these students in a new light, they provided more praise and encouragement, both privately and publicly. Moreover, other students in the class treated them differently. For instance, the fourth-grade student referred to above discovered that other students in the class spontaneously clustered around his computer, cheered him on, and marveled at his accomplishment. The teacher subsequently provided him with a certificate for being the first to complete the intricate puzzle. The teacher commented, "He left the room beaming. Anytime I can do this for a kid it's so worthwhile."

Changes in Classroom Strategies

Once teachers recognized the benefits of student collaboration and peer tutoring, they made simple alterations in their classrooms to take full advantage of student expertise. At one site, for example, teachers decided to combine their fifth and sixth grades for some activities to allow students the opportunity to teach each other. Once again, teachers reported seeing their lower-achieving students in a new light:

> What's neat about this is that the kids who don't normally shine are helping those older and sometimes more accomplished. The ideas trickle down through the kids—they show me what they're doing on the computer and we all learn.

Other elementary teachers organized some of their lessons so that pairs of students could work together on the computers:

> When two kids are working on a computer, which is sometimes how I have them organized and working, the cliché "two heads are better than one" comes in. When they are working on a new piece of software, they help each other with it, they answer each other's questions, and they seem to figure things out together easier.

At the high school site, teachers felt concern that new students would have difficulty keeping up with their older, more computer-literate peers. To provide the new students with the additional assistance they needed, they combined ninth- and tenth-grade students in study hall "to see what spontaneous interactions may occur." Teachers also assigned students' seats with peer tutoring in mind. As one of the coordinators commented:

> ACOT teachers did a great job of arranging the seating chart in the sophomore class so that each new student is close to one or two students from last year that fit their personalities and will be the most helpful. The peer tutoring really takes the pressure off the teachers to try to do everything.

Teachers increasingly noticed benefits of student collaboration and interaction brought about by the introduction of technology to their classrooms. As it became apparent that both teachers and classmates could profit from the knowledge and expertise of some students, teachers expanded their use of student experts.

EXPANDING THE ROLE OF STUDENT EXPERTS

Over time, the role of student experts took on two new dimensions. First, students began to share their expertise with a variety of people beyond the ACOT classrooms. Second, teachers allowed students to teach one another subject matter content in addition to technological information.

A Changing Audience for Student Expertise

Besides assisting their peers and ACOT teachers, students began sharing their technical expertise at home and reaching out to others at school and in the community. At home, students often became the family's technical expert. For example, one teacher commented that a girl in her class had to help her father make their home computer operational, "despite his continuous references to the manual." Other students reportedly taught family members to use database programs or spreadsheets, or tutored siblings using the home computers. At one site children used computers to help their parents learn to read.

At school, students began instructing younger students, administrators, retired community members, non-ACOT teachers within the school, and even substitute teachers about technology. One student, for example, showed the principal at her school how to use the electronic bulletin board. When a substitute teacher wanted to type a letter, several high school students taught her how to use a word-processing application. Some students spent time after school helping teachers who were not involved with the project learn about the technology:

> The art teacher came in to have a student show him the drawing program on the computer. The typing teacher . . . wants to work with a student who can show her about word processing. It is an excellent opportunity for both these teachers and the students.

By the end of the project's second year, even the school district valued the high school students' technological expertise. The district hired students as technical support people to help set up equipment and to serve as teaching assistants in summer courses for district personnel. Teachers at the high school level began taking students' technological expertise for granted, forgetting that student-led classroom presentations on computer applications were not commonplace occurrences:

> What impressed our visitor the most was all the teachers coming into the room, taking the handouts and watching the students' presentations [on computer applications] and really learning something. We're so used to student-led presentations now, we just assume that a teacher who wants to learn would take advantage of these presentations, but the visitor's fresh viewpoint showed me that maybe this doesn't happen everywhere.

Finally, both elementary and high school ACOT students discovered audiences for their skills beyond their classrooms, districts, and homes. One elementary group was invited several times to create technology classrooms in a shopping mall to help more community members understand technology. Three years in a row, teachers and students from another site traveled to the state capitol where they set up their classroom at the annual state fair. Other students shared their knowledge at an industry symposium and at numerous state and national conferences. Community firms hired high school students as technology consultants. And, perhaps most unique, a group of fourth-graders and high school students accompanied by their teachers testified before the Congressional Subcommittee on Space, Science, and Technology in Washington, D.C.

Students as Subject Matter Experts

The role of student experts was further augmented when teachers began to allow them to present subject matter content to the class. At first, this occurred infrequently, and often resulted from a teacher taking advantage of a "teachable moment" rather than being planned:

> We are covering the Civil War . . . After we covered some of the battles, a couple of students came up and told me about a Civil War battle that happened around the high school area. I asked them if they would do some research on it and present it to the class . . . I'm excited because I never knew that information . . . I've had students come up and tell me things before but I have

not seen them go out and do research on it. This was from two students in the classroom who are not the best students.

Eventually, teachers at the high school level began planning entire units in which the students, rather than the teacher, presented the content to be learned.

> Last year when I was away from school, I told the kids to figure out how to teach Chapter 6 so they could teach it when I returned. This year I'll be here, but I'm trying the same approach . . . I'll let them choose what method to use to present.

Teachers typically found that this student-centered instructional approach took more time than the traditional format, but they felt that the time was well spent.

> Last week we did our fifties project . . . I learned some things from students about animation and the computers. I really enjoyed this project because of the fact that I learned a lot and it really gave the students a chance to show their creativity . . . We had planned two days for presentations and it took four days, but the quality of the presentations was unbelievable. The presentations together taught the class about the fifties. It made my job a lot easier.

In some math and chemistry classes, teachers abandoned the traditional stand-up-and-lecture mode of instruction. Instead, they asked students to coach one another. One wrote that "students gathered in areas and were coached by their classmates wearing badges that designated problems that they were expert on . . . I was a coach like the students." Another teacher described his approach:

> I list the number of specific problems missed by students in the class on the chalkboard. Students who got the problem right and feel that they can explain the rationale for their answer place their names on the board under that problem. Students who missed the problem then have a resource person to ask questions if they can't understand why they missed the problem . . . It is amazing how excited both classes are about this approach and it saves me from having to stand up in front and go over each problem as I did when I taught in the traditional program.

CONSIDERATIONS IN REDEFINING CLASSROOM ROLES

Research in traditional classrooms and in the ACOT project indicate that increasing peer interaction and student collaboration has many benefits. The remainder of this chapter briefly reviews findings of other studies related to peer collaboration and highlights several issues that should be considered when using this instructional strategy.

Peer interaction and student collaboration have been extensively investigated in traditional classroom settings. Formalized systems of peer tutoring and collaboration vary: one approach pairs experienced students with relative novices (Dedicott, 1986); another combines relative novices who have roughly the same level of competence (Ames & Murray, 1982); and another divides children into heterogeneous teams of five or six who work both individually and together on a task (Slavin, 1983). Researchers have found that peer learning can enhance academic achievement in a variety of domains, such as writing (Reed, 1990), mathematical and spatial reasoning (Phelps & Damon, 1989), reading (Atherley, 1989), and foreign language (Chesterfield & Chesterfield, 1985). Peer learning has also been found to increase students' self-esteem and social status (Maheady & Sainato, 1985), as well as their motivation and self-direction (Land, 1984).

Our research indicates that student collaboration has similar benefits in technology-rich classrooms. Initially reluctant and uncertain, teachers gradually gained confidence in the advantages of student collaboration. Their change in thinking became evident through the increasing frequency of collaborative opportunities for students, the move toward allowing them to serve as subject-matter experts, and the use of students for tutoring beyond the classroom walls.

Numerous benefits from using cadres of student experts emerged. Spontaneous peer tutoring freed teachers from repeating basic information and made learning more personal as students helped each other one on one. Teachers noticed positive changes in students' self-efficacy and academic performance. Perhaps most important in the long run, teachers, administrators, and parents changed their perceptions about children's capacities and talents. Most rewarding are stories about those who have been perceived as slow or reluctant learners, emerging as children with promise when given an alternative avenue for the expression of their knowledge.

When teachers use peer tutoring and collaborative student groups, several considerations should be taken into account. First, teachers often think that their more advanced students will best serve as experts. Our research illustrates numerous advantages when lower-achieving students take on the role of expert. Not only do teachers, peers, and family members see these students in a different light, but the experience often enhances the student expert's self-esteem. Second, students should not be limited to sharing their expertise only with their peers. Teachers, administrators, parents, and siblings can all learn from student experts.

Third, the students' forms of instruction further demonstrate the power of the "apprenticeship of observation" (Lortie, 1975). When ACOT students were teaching each other how to use the technology—a skill with which they had little experience in schools—hands-on instruction was the norm. However, when they began to deliver content information to one another, they typically taught as they had been taught. Earlier, one teacher succinctly captured the problem with many student presentations: "Most of the students taught the way I probably teach now—too much talking." To be more effective, student experts will need to be provided with teaching techniques that go beyond the traditional lecture–recitation–seat work model.

Fourth, as teachers move toward models of teaching that include high levels of peer collaboration, traditional forms of assessment may not be adequate. When students are allowed to share information openly with one another, customary forms of measuring student knowledge and achievement may not suffice. For instance, teachers using collaborative groups indicate that they often have difficulty monitoring individual students' contributions. When technology is added to the picture, assessment becomes even more complicated.

The following excerpt exemplifies the assessment dilemma facing teachers who are learning how to use technology and trying to adapt to higher levels of peer interaction. A teacher unfamiliar with computers was working closely with an ACOT teacher in a physics lab. The ACOT students were helping their non-ACOT peers learn how to use spreadsheets for data collection. The ACOT teacher described his colleague's concerns in his audiotape journal:

> We have a veteran teacher over there who has 27 or 28 years of teaching experience and has never used computers in his classroom. He said, "I'm a little afraid of this whole thing." I said, "Well, the kids know what's going on." He said, "Yeah, that's the scary part—they know what's going on, and I'm not sure I know how to evaluate it."

A study investigating assessment in ACOT's technology-intensive classrooms (Gearhart, Herman, Baker, & Novak, 1990) suggests that students who are the most successful at peer tutoring or at demonstrating technological expertise to others typically do not have the highest grade-point averages in their classrooms. Although teachers' pride in these student experts is evident in weekly links and audiotapes—and in the verbal support they provide to these students—teachers do not know how to translate students' teaching skills into a grade on a standard report card. Clearly, development and dissemination of alternative assessment techniques are necessary so that these teachers can more accurately measure and describe their students' progress.

6

Maintaining Student Engagement

Students are answering questions from the board on their computers . . . The attention that they direct to their work is much greater than before we had the computers. There's just no comparison. They are much more attentive and enthusiastic. There is almost total silence once they begin work, versus when they were writing everything out . . . I can really see a difference.

As Marge Austen, a high school teacher, just described, the introduction of technology into project classrooms generated an enthusiastic response from both students and teachers. Although teachers welcomed increases in student initiative, time spent on projects, experimentation, and on-task behavior, their students' enthusiasm for using technology sometimes led to difficulties for teachers—such as disruption of planned activities, students overstepping boundaries with respect to assignments, and time tradeoffs. This chapter examines these changes in student engagement, describing both the positive changes and the accompanying challenges.

POSITIVE CHANGES IN STUDENT ENGAGEMENT

As the ACOT project progressed, teachers saw students become more excited about learning, and their excitement was contagious. Their enthusiasm aided student learning and reinforced teachers' efforts. Students displayed increased initiative by going beyond requirements of assignments and by independently experimenting with and exploring new applications. Students spent more time on assignments and projects when working on computers, and they chose to use the computers during free-time and after-school hours. The next section describes these positive changes.

Changes in Student Attitude

Early in the project, teachers noted the marked enthusiasm of their students when working with computers. Teachers described students' excitement, their awe at learning new software programs, and their disappointment at not having more time on the computers. One elementary teacher compared a new piece of software to a new Christmas toy—with children nagging until they got to use it.

This high level of enthusiasm held a number of benefits for both teachers and students. Students learned more quickly when they were anxious to learn, and their interest reinforced teachers' efforts. After commenting on students who were "ecstatic" and "absolutely beside themselves," one teacher reflected: "Their enthusiasm is well worth the effort it has taken to set up a file server."

ACOT teachers compared the new attitudes of their students to their attitudes before the addition of computers to their classrooms. For example, a high school teacher commented about how his students' interest and motivation typically extended into the last week of school—an uncommon occurrence before the project began. Over the years of the project, he remembered only two or three instances where students turned in their home computers a few days early. The majority of the students in the project, including seniors who had been using computers for their entire high school careers, kept their home computers until the last possible day. Some elementary students requested a make-up session for a day when a field trip caused them to miss a computer club session. Another teacher noticed differences in students' journal entries; one student described spelling as "fun," and another declared, "A computer a day keeps the blues away."

When a high school teacher put together a second course in computer applications, he hoped that about 10 students would sign up, but he ended up with a class of 34. After writing some music on a synthesizer with three students during study hall, another high school teacher found that "it became a desirable thing for students to work on the synthesizers during study hall." The comment by an elementary teacher probably sums it up best: "The students don't get tired of working on the computer. They actually ask for things to do. In all of my years of teaching, I never had anyone ask for another ditto." When given the choice, students often chose the computer over pencil and paper for writing assignments, test taking, and even artwork. Teachers also found students more willing to edit their written work. Teachers expressed particular pleasure when students eventually began to edit on their own, making changes spontaneously.

The enthusiasm of individual students motivated other students in the class. For instance, a fourth-grade student who had finished his work asked to use a disk that he had found on a shelf. It turned out to be a mathematics program on multiplication that the teacher had never previewed. Before long, the teacher had a large group of students eager to "get their hands on it." The motivational power of peers exceeds that of teachers. In the words of another elementary teacher: "It's incredible—you get a few people who seem to pick the program up and think it's great, and all of sudden the whole class does."

Through their work on computers, some students developed talents and skills that led to jobs in their communities. For example, a sixth-grader developed enough proficiency with spreadsheets to develop a bookkeeping system for his mother's import business. When word of his accomplishment spread through his small town, the local bank asked him to help set up a spreadsheet program. In another community, businesses hired high school students to design templates because of the students' knowledge of spreadsheets, word processing, and desktop publishing. At one school, the students' interest in and dedication to a tabloid student publication led to summer jobs and job interviews. As the teacher commented:

> I'm very happy with the work we're doing on this publication—40 pages, tabloid size, three colors, borders, color separation with clip art, over 300 advertisements with very detailed proof-reading required. The man at the press that is doing the printing is very impressed with the quality of the work. He has offered summer jobs to some of the kids and wants to talk about job possibilities with any who may not be going on to college.

In addition, the Center for Science and Industry wanted to hire ACOT students from the high school to help build a simulation for a "Mission to Mars" project. Students' experiences in ACOT class-rooms allowed them to develop job skills that they otherwise might not have learned.

Fascination with computers extended to students not involved in the program. At an elementary school, teachers frequently discovered various first-grade students "on their knees, under tables in the centrum peering into the ACOT classroom." The site coordinator assumed that the children were intrigued by the male teacher, one of only two in the entire school. However, after questioning some of the "peeping toms," she learned that it was the computers attracting their attention.

Changes in Time Usage

As students became involved in working on computers, the time they spent on assignments and projects often increased. Teachers discov-ered, for example, that the 30 minutes they had allotted for an activity stretched into an hour, or even an entire afternoon. As a teacher sum-marized, "Once you get something that piques everyone's interest, you let them run with it." One teacher reported even running over into another teacher's class time, explaining, "I just couldn't cut them off."

Moreover, when given free time, students chose to work on com-puters rather than on other activities. As one parent of an elementary student observed, the children never seemed to be able to work on the computer for as long as they wanted. In fact, in a second-grade classroom, students asked for more time on the computers following a Halloween party.

In some classrooms, students also came in before and after school to work on the computers. Teachers initially found it surprising when students stayed through recesses and lunch periods to work with technology. Whereas their students had previously been anxious for school to end, ACOT teachers discovered that students voluntarily requested to stay after school. As one teacher stated, "We are using some cooperative software now that the kids love. When we use it toward the end of the day, the kids don't want to go home. That didn't happen in a traditional classroom." At one site, after a number of indoor recesses due to rain, students became upset when the teacher announced outside recess. When questioned about their response, the students indicated that they had hoped to stay in and work on the computers.

Teachers also found it unusual that students would stay after school for questions and activities related to instruction rather than more typical extracurricular activities. For example, one high school teacher indicated that she had never been at a school where students were interested in coming in after school or during their study hall periods to do work: "What I have experienced is students getting out of study hall to play." Another teacher describes an incident where a high school student engaged a visiting researcher in conversation about a programming language:

> Tim is not one of the designated students for the research, but Tim stayed after class when the researcher was here recently just to talk to him about a programming language. Do you know how unusual it is for a student to stay after class to discuss content?

After years of experience in classrooms, ACOT teachers viewed students' degree of commitment and engagement as "unusual in a group of quite ordinary kids." As one teacher commented:

> We've had a great time using this software program! The kids are extremely enthusiastic and productive. I needed to go to a lunch meeting today, and they didn't want me to go because they were still working and wanted to know more. How often do you see kids working through lunch? It's fantastic!

At some sites, before-school sessions eventually became formalized. One site coordinator pointed out that 24 out of 27 elementary students faithfully came to school one hour early each morning to provide time "to work in all of the things we want to do."

A number of parents also commented to teachers about the amount of time their children spent working on home computers.

Parents expressed pleasure that the computer could lure their children away from the television. The comments of the following parent typify their responses:

> Since this class has been in existence, John has . . . a phenomenal interest in computers. Instead of wanting to always watch television or go outside and play, John can be found at his computer a large part of the time trying to learn more and more about programming.

Changes in Student On-Task Behavior

Teachers reported that students' enthusiasm and interest resulted in greater on-task behavior. They found that students, during computer activities, were highly involved in their assignments and frequently able to work with little assistance. Teachers sometimes expressed surprise at the level of students' interest: "This was probably the first time I've ever seen a whole group of students with actually every student on task and excited about their learning."

A high school teacher who taught both regular ninth-grade classes and ACOT ninth-grade classes described differences she observed in students' behavior.

> The ninth-grade classes I teach are entirely different; they are like night and day. The ACOT students are constantly working. They always have the computers on. They always want to see their work right away. I have never seen students who want to work so much.

Another high school teacher was amazed at how industrious his students were right before Christmas break. Similarly, at the end of the school year, when most teachers were winding down and gathering materials, teachers in ACOT classrooms were still beginning new activities. According to one of the elementary school coordinators, "The students showed no signs of quitting either, so the education process just kept humming along."

Visitors and substitutes also commented on the high interest and engagement of students. For instance, a visitor to one of the high school classrooms noted that he saw some students doing five things at once and still paying attention. Other visitors seemed surprised that students stayed on task with strangers roaming through the classroom. One substitute teacher made the following comparisons between ACOT science classes and regular science classes:

> All students in the ACOT classroom were aware of what they were supposed to be doing. Their attitude was positive, and they showed in many ways that they were following the lesson AND had a high interest in what they were doing. They kept their level of effort up for the whole period . . . The same attention span is not evident in the regular science classes . . . In the regular class many had trouble just concentrating on what they were doing. The interest level was just not there in doing their assignment. Most were unable to complete the entire assignment. If they didn't get the answer, they just left it blank. In the ACOT class, the questions the students were asking each other had to do with the lesson, while during the regular class, at least half the questions were social or something outside the lesson.

Teachers also discovered that students who did not do well in a typical setting frequently excelled when working with technology. Low achievers had a chance to experience success and began concentrating and applying themselves to their projects (see Chapter 5).

Changes in Student Initiative

Increases in student initiative occurred in two ways. First, many students went beyond the requirements of their assignments. Teachers reported that students volunteered to do work on the computer beyond the teachers' expectations. For example, on their own, high school chemistry students developed a spreadsheet to do the calculations for an assignment. In a first-grade classroom, students decided to compile their stories into a book with illustrations. As part of an election project, high school students developed a computerized voter registration system complete with sound.

Second, individual students or small groups of students independently explored new applications and developed skills; their activities then spontaneously attracted the interest of other students in the class. For instance, students created spreadsheets on their own for everything from baseball cards to paper-route billings. Several sixth-grade boys used a hypermedia application to independently create a computer adventure game. In a second-grade classroom, a student asked to share a story he had written on his home computer. His story created a wave of interest among the students in the class. As the project coordinator describes, "The boys formed a mystery-story writers group, complete with a name. They ask to have free time to write their stories. They even went to the publishing center to make an appointment to bind their books."

Increased Student Experimentation and Risk Taking

The students' enhanced engagement while using technology led to greater experimentation by the students, which in turn increased their level of engagement even further. Working independently with computers, students seemed willing to take more risks. Through this experimentation, they learned and discovered new applications without direct instruction.

Through experimentation, students could explore new programs and applications without concern about making mistakes. As one teacher commented, "They get to practice in private with the computer, which doesn't really judge, and nobody keeps a record or a tally of what's going on." Moreover, with computers, when students found out that a particular strategy didn't succeed, they generally would keep working independently until they figured it out on their own. In contrast, when working with a teacher, students could directly ask for an answer about what to do next, thus inhibiting their inclination to discover solutions on their own.

One teacher also observed that, unlike many adults, students seemed unafraid of "crashing or causing any problems"; this attitude enhanced their desire to "try everything." At one site, a coordinator walked into a classroom and was immediately mobbed with students—"not with inquiries for help, as might be expected with the introduction of software, but rather with pleas to see what each of them had discovered on their own."

Taking advantage of students' experimentation and engagement, teachers could introduce an assignment and then focus their efforts on individual students or small-group activities such as directed reading. The opportunity to experiment and explore also enhanced student creativity. Students frequently came up with ideas that teachers had never considered, often leading teachers to seek technical help to follow through on their ideas.

CHALLENGES ASSOCIATED WITH CHANGES IN STUDENT ENGAGEMENT

Although ACOT teachers viewed changes in student engagement as primarily positive, the changes produced challenges for them. Teachers wondered to what extent students should be allowed to go beyond assignments and questioned amounts of time spent on computer activities. Teachers found it difficult to move students to other classroom activities and frequently found their plans disrupted. Student enthusiasm turned to frustration when software programs were used repeatedly and when computer assignments were too easy or too difficult. In addition, some students had difficulty adjusting to computerized environments with increased noise, sharing among students, and simultaneous activities. In this section we elaborate on these challenges.

Problems with Student Frustration

Increased student enthusiasm led to numerous benefits, but it also created concerns for teachers. When educational software programs were used repeatedly or when computer projects were too difficult or too easy, students' enthusiasm turned to frustration. The same programs used day after day became routine and boring. As one teacher put it, "We have observed how you can lose them if you don't keep them extremely motivated. If a piece of software gets old to them, they won't stick with it." A high school teacher pointed out that students started to tire of a particular tool software program because they were using it in all subject areas.

ACOT teachers also began to recognize that some software programs created a great deal of initial enthusiasm but couldn't sustain student interest for more than a few days. For example, students lost interest in software that was directed and didn't allow for sufficient experimentation. The students preferred to explore rather than be told how to do something, whether by a computer or a human. When new software was being introduced, students got bored with the guided tours included in programs but perked up again when they were allowed to investigate and discover on their own.

Particular computer programs and projects proved too difficult for some students, yet too easy for others in the same class. For example, slow readers quickly became frustrated with complex computer programs, and students who had trouble with vocabulary lost interest in programs that focused on word games. Students who could quickly sail through a program also became bored and frustrated if not given additional challenges.

Time Tradeoffs

As students became more interested in learning while using technology, they began to have trouble managing their time. Teachers sometimes questioned whether they should allow computer activities to extend beyond the allotted time. One teacher finally instructed a student teacher to stop waiting for students to finish working at the computer because "they would be at the computer all day if given the choice."

Additionally, teachers expressed concern about students' large investments of time on items such as layout or cover design for a project. They wondered if time spent on making the project visually appealing detracted from time spent on content. As one teacher noted, "Some of the students get bogged down in the artwork and spend hours drawing things. Of course, it's a lot more fun to draw rather than dig out the difficult parts of the section to be presented." Another teacher who was learning to integrate multimedia into her classroom worried about the "glitz versus the guts of students' projects."

Finally, some teachers and parents questioned the tradeoff of time for physical and social activities. For example, an elementary teacher felt that students needed time at recess to be outside and to learn to socialize with each other, and, similarly, a parent worried that her son was becoming "a computer nerd."

Increased Student Distractions

Despite the positive effect of technology on most students' level of engagement, teachers continued to be challenged by some students' off-task behavior. For instance, some students became distracted by the noise of printers and keyboards, and of their classmates moving freely around the classroom. Although most students adapted to the technology-rich environment, others seemed unable to handle sharing among students and various activities going on simultaneously. An elementary teacher believed that "the child who is off task with pencil and paper is off task on the computer, and maybe more so because of the many distractions going on around him with technology." Another elementary teacher prohibited game-type learning programs in class because students became so noisy and excited when using them.

Teachers also puzzled over some students' unwillingness to complete homework assignments on their home computers. For example, a team of sixth-grade teachers reported how students had been "itching to do something on their own [home] computer"; but only 27 out of 71 students completed the first assignment. A fourth-grade teacher couldn't understand why some of her students would "work [on their computers] at school but do very little at home." A high school teacher became discouraged by a group of seniors who were "not completing any homework assignments."

Although the time students voluntarily spent on computer projects far exceeded the typical 20-minute attention span of elementary students, teachers discovered that students had a saturation point. In one unusual circumstance, when elementary students worked on computers for six hours as part of a videotaping project, one said, "I never thought I would get tired of the computer, but I don't care if I don't see one for a while." The point at which students began to lose their concentration varied across individuals and depended on the type of computer assignment. An elementary school project coordinator observed that minor off-task behavior started after students had been working for one-and-a-half hours on a computer project.

Problems with Setting Boundaries

While teachers generally appreciated and encouraged the increase in students' willingness to go beyond the requirements of their assignments and their independence while exploring new applications, they also had to grapple with the question of boundaries. As one teacher described, "Sometimes the kids get ahead of us. The question is, Do we let them go or do we hold them back a little bit?" The response to this query varied across teachers. Some teachers reported having "to keep the kids from going too far," others accepted the situation, and still others purposely developed assignments that allowed students with the interest and ability to go beyond minimum requirements.

For example, after completing a unit on spreadsheets, one high school teacher discovered a student creating a spreadsheet for compiling price quotes and bids from various companies. This task was not an assignment; she was "doing this as an exercise to help out her brother who was taking a college class on spreadsheets." Rather than discourage her, the teacher helped her a little bit and had her give a short demonstration to the class. Similarly, in a fifth-grade classroom where students were "really stretching the boundaries of the software," the teacher supported students' initiative by calling the software-assistance hotline to determine the feasibility of students' ideas. In another elementary classroom, the teacher gave a short assignment on time-ordered paragraphs:

> I had envisioned this to be a short assignment with a simple
> topic, but a number of the kids tackled long, involved subjects . . .
> One student wrote a paragraph on the life cycle of the penguin,

but then he expanded it and took parts of his paragraph and wrote a treatise on how to write a time-ordered paragraph. He used his paragraph as an example. It was a wonderful piece of writing about three or four pages long.

As student-centered, self-directed learning became common-place, ACOT teachers needed to consider carefully the issue of setting boundaries to avoid limiting student ambition. When teachers found the right balance between freedom and control, they were gratified by the result. As one ACOT teacher reflected, "I was really pleased with the way these kids are taking risks and going beyond what is expected of them and being able to explore. They are more imaginative and creative in their thinking."

Disruption of Teacher Plans

Student experimentation with computers also presented challenges to teachers, particularly with respect to classroom plans. Students often became so engrossed in their work on the computers that they ignored other assignments or continued to work when they should have been listening. For example, when working with new functions, such as visual effects, sounds effects or scanners, students wanted to stick with their experimentation until they solved their problem. When one teacher tried reorganizing the schedule so that the intro-duction of new software followed another assignment, she noted that some students became clock-watchers. She went on to say, "The stu-dents are so eager to get into some of the computer programs that they aren't taking other classwork seriously. Somehow I have to com-municate to them that there is a time for everything and each thing has its place." Certain software programs held such appeal that many teachers eventually monitored and limited their use. One teacher, after attending a workshop, developed greater empathy toward stu-dents' difficulty in moving to other classroom activities. As he describes:

> I notice it is hard for the kids to break away when I say "Stop!" in class, too. Recently I found myself doing the same kind of thing during a software workshop. I just kept right on showing some-body something when the presenter asked for our attention.

Teachers varied in their reactions to the disruption of their plans. Some teachers viewed it as a significant problem, while others saw it as a potent opportunity for learning.

TOWARD A BROADER VIEW OF STUDENT ENGAGEMENT

Teachers, administrators, parents, and researchers alike agree on the importance of student engagement. When students are actively engaged and involved in a meaningful task, learning is a likely result.

Researchers investigating student engagement often rely on proxy measures such as "time on task." Here a student's rate of engagement is determined using observable behavioral measures such as whether the student is gazing out the window or looking at the teacher while he or she is talking. In these studies, outside observers decide if a student "is looking at some appropriate instructional object or person" (Wilson, 1987, p. 15) for 5 or 10 seconds of each minute during a short segment of the school day (MacArthur, Haynes, & Malouf, 1986; Magliaro & Borko, 1986; McGarity & Butts, 1984). These types of measures, however, provide little useful information for teachers anxious to increase student engagement.

Frequent responses to these time-on-task studies are new policies aimed at lengthening the school day and specifying time allocations for various subject areas. Although well intentioned, these approaches ignore the larger instructional picture and may lead to greater student *disengagement* if teaching practices remain unchanged. By looking at student engagement more broadly and over longer periods of time, we can begin to find conditions that support it.

In our work, teachers, rather than researchers, determined whether students were engaged. Unlike outside observers, who typically make inferences based on brief observations of unfamiliar students, teachers know how much time and effort individual students devote to different tasks and how their level of engagement changes from day to day and from month to month as the academic year progresses. When learning activities extend over hours, days, and weeks, it is meaningless to measure engagement in terms of seconds and minutes, as researchers typically do in time-on-task studies. In our study, we considered student engagement to include variables such as initiative, self-motivation, independent experimentation, spontaneous collaboration and peer coaching, and enthusiasm or frustration. In addition, we included not only on-task behavior in school but also time spent on projects both in and out of classrooms.

Many educational reforms are consistent with a broader view of student engagement. For example, the California Elementary Grades Task Force recommends reducing the amount of time spent on skill-based activities in favor of authentic learning tasks based on discovery and active student participation (California Department of Education, 1992). Although "the traditional skills-based curriculum lent itself to short blocks of time for each subject area," the thinking curriculum requires "longer blocks of time—extending over not just several hours but over days or even weeks of effort" (p. 26). The California High School Task Force points to the need for flexible use of time, driven by the curriculum and controlled by an interdisciplinary team of teachers (California Department of Education, 1992). The premise underlying these recommendations is that students' schoolwork must be "interesting and engaging" (p. 29). Instructional practices that are interdisciplinary, student centered, and project based require a change in how educators evaluate student engagement.

CONDITIONS FOR CREATING ENDURING STUDENT ENGAGEMENT

Although various studies indicate that technology has a positive impact on student engagement (Bright, 1988; Johnston & Joscelyn, 1989; Latham & Stoddard, 1986; MacArthur, Haynes, & Malouf, 1986; Mevarech, 1986; Perkins, 1988; Zuk & Danner, 1986), these increases are often attributed to the novelty effect (Fish & Feldman, 1988; Hawkins, Sheingold, Gearhart, & Berger, 1982). By looking at the long-term impact of technology on student engagement, our research shows that the critical factor is not the novelty of the computer but rather how technology is being used in classroom instruction. In the ACOT classrooms, technology became an integral part of classroom life rather than an unusual, add-on feature to the curriculum that students used for a few minutes every week. While the initial enthusiasm that technology generates may cause teachers to believe that student engagement will increase indefinitely, overall instructional practices are pivotal. Students can be disengaged just as quickly with technology as with traditional instruction. Drill-and-practice exercises on the computer differ very little from drill-and-practice exercises on paper.

We found that technology had an enduring, positive impact on student engagement in classrooms only under certain conditions. First, in classrooms where teachers used technology as one tool among many in their instructional repertoire, students were less likely to reach a saturation point on computers. In such classrooms, teachers used computers only when they were the most *appropriate* tool for completing an assignment, not simply because they were available.

Second, student engagement remained high in classrooms where technology use was integrated into the larger curricular framework. Learning how to use technology was not viewed by ACOT teachers as another subject to fit into an already full curriculum, as so often happens in schools with computer labs. Teachers who allowed students to learn computer skills within the context of a meaningful assignment—rather than setting aside a block of "computer time" where students would practice keyboarding or learn how to do word processing—were generally rewarded with higher levels of student engagement.

Third, student engagement was more likely to endure in classrooms that emphasized the use of tool applications such as word-processing programs, desktop-publishing software, and hypermedia applications. While drill-and-practice software had its place in some classrooms, overreliance on materials such as these generally led to student boredom and frustration before too long. Students were most engaged when using programs that allowed experimentation and exploration, processes not fostered by most drill-and-practice software.

Fourth, student engagement was fostered in classrooms where teachers adjusted the use of technology to individual differences in both interest and ability. Just as students will lose interest in a mathematics assignment that is too simple or too difficult, so too will they become frustrated when using technology if teachers do not take their individual needs into account.

Finally, many of the dilemmas that ACOT teachers faced related more to their beliefs about traditional teacher roles than to problems inherent to using technology in the classroom. For example, in classrooms where teachers were willing to relinquish their role as dispenser of knowledge and allowed students more control over their own learning, concerns about issues such as overzealous student experimentation and disruption of teacher plans became less paramount than in classrooms that remained more teacher directed. And, as teachers moved away from the belief that they had to break learning up into discrete subject areas such as mathematics and language, they started relying more on project-based instruction and became less concerned that the computer was taking away time from other subject areas. Thus, dilemmas brought about by the introduction of technology challenged teachers to reexamine beliefs about their classroom roles. Fundamental instructional changes such as these have a positive impact on student engagement far more lasting than any technological tool in and of itself.

7

Enhancing Innovation and Promoting Collegial Sharing: A Reciprocal Relationship

❝ We have all grown a lot in this program because we are usually not asked to work together like this in our profession . . . But one team member is really a problem . . . Gary is an extremely difficult team player—selfish, self-centered, and stubborn . . . I don't know if there have been problems like this at other sites but it can really break a team up. ❞

During a period of reflection, Theresa Barton points out highs and lows of working closely together in a team. Teacher isolation, a common feature in school settings, inhibits collegial sharing and teacher growth. Yet, as Ms. Barton discovered, the formation of teams is not a quick cure. Although collegial sharing offers many benefits to teachers and students, the process of building collaboration is slow and filled with obstacles.

In addition to the organizational supports built into ACOT (see Chapter 3), teachers benefited from the collegiality that developed among them as a result of their participation in the project. Technology-rich ACOT classrooms drove teachers to engage in more collegial sharing to prepare for their classes and update their curriculum. The reverse was also evident: Teachers in schools with a high level of collegial sharing tended to embrace technology and implement new instructional strategies more quickly. At the beginning of the project, teacher interaction was infrequent and focused on emotional support. Over time, their interactions shifted to include technical assistance, instructional sharing, and, eventually, formalized team teaching. In this chapter we examine the changes in collegial sharing among ACOT teachers that were prompted by the technology-rich classrooms and discuss the relationship between instructional change and collegial sharing. Finally, we summarize research and raise issues related to educational innovation and teacher collaboration.

CHANGES IN COLLEGIAL SHARING

As the ACOT project progressed, changes in the frequency and form of collegial sharing among the teachers became evident. Table 7.1 summarizes the main differences within the categories of collegial sharing.

Emotional Support

During the first months of the project, teachers had little time for collegial sharing, even though ACOT provided supports for such interaction—professional release time, training workshops, and a telecommunications network between sites. As the year progressed, the frequency of interaction among teachers increased. However, exchanges remained informal, providing primarily emotional support. ACOT teachers shared their frustrations and successes as they

Table 7.1 Categories of collegial sharing

Emotional support	Sharing frustrations and successes
	Providing encouragement
Technical assistance	Managing equipment
	Using equipment
	Locating software
	Using software
	Dealing with technical problems
Instructional sharing	Discussing instructional strategies
	Sharing ideas
	Observing instruction
Team teaching	Joint planning
	Developing curriculum
	Teaching together
	Interdisciplinary teaching

dealt with rooms full of computers, cables, and children. The following excerpt exemplifies the nature of their exchanges:

> I am still concerned with the noise level. What is best? . . . It bothers me and frustrates me, and I would love to discuss this with others. HELP! What do others do about this? Today I more or less let the noise go because the teams were so engrossed in their work.

Technical Assistance

As teachers began to use new technology in their instruction, their collegial sharing increased but revolved around providing technical assistance. Teachers in ACOT classrooms, both within and across sites, shared strategies in areas such as managing equipment and locating relevant software. For instance, one teacher who was looking for software specific to geometry sent the following query:

> Susan has been working on geometry and measurement in math. She is using [a particular software program] to demonstrate concepts. The students have really taken to it, since they think they are playing. Does anyone have any software that can be used to teach geometry?

Formal meetings of project teachers at each site provided opportunities for sharing experiences and ideas. Teachers also started to make more frequent use of weekly reports and the telecommunications network to communicate with teachers at other sites. Technical assistance was not limited to technological concerns but extended to other areas, such as dealing with student misbehavior. For instance, one teacher describes the assistance she received from another teacher for solving a problem:

> I found out that the kids had put their database information together, and I saw the same entries in my combined database. Unfortunately, I didn't know which student did what entries because I just dumped all of the files into my database. Peter told me how I can put the student's name in a column and then know what data belongs to what student.

Teachers with less computer expertise approached their colleagues for assistance and capitalized on opportunities to learn from each other:

> At this point, I must say I am feeling a little overwhelmed and will probably continue to feel this way for some time to come. I learned some things this summer, but there is so much more to learn . . . I have been attending Anne's computer applications class and will continue to attend the rest of the year.

Technical assistance among teachers helped them to adopt the new technology and to begin to use it in their instruction, even if simply as a support for their previous instructional style. Conversely, because teachers began to accept the innovation, they had questions and concerns that compelled them to seek assistance from their colleagues.

Instructional Sharing

As teachers began to integrate technology into their instruction, the substance of their interactions shifted from offering technical assistance to sharing teaching strategies. Collaboration about instructional topics emerged when teachers ventured beyond using technology for text-based, drill-and-practice instruction. Their experimentation with new instructional strategies motivated them to share their endeavors with other teachers and sites, as the following excerpt illustrates:

> The kids are transposing their music on the computer. We then got into doing shapes, which resulted in animation. We're using a different software program for graphics and animation, also including sound effects. The kids love it; they worked solidly at it. It was amazing what they all came up with; they work in cooperative groups so no one gets left out. I'd like to share this with another site that has a sixth grade. I'd like to get more communication between our classrooms.

The telecommunications network permitted ACOT teachers to communicate across sites and receive prompt answers to their queries. But not all instructional sharing across sites occurred as a result of direct questions. For example, all participating teachers had the opportunity to read weekly reports submitted by each site. Doing so frequently led to unsolicited offers of assistance among teachers:

> I just read your weekly and noticed you'd be doing an auto-biography. I wrote up an autobiography unit for my lesson last year and would be willing to pass it along to you if you think it would be any help. We're having all our fifth- and sixth-graders write them this year based on this plan. Let me know.

As teachers began to feel comfortable with increased interaction, they started to *observe* each other teaching rather than simply discuss their instructional ideas. Previously, very few teachers had observed other classrooms, and when they did, the primary purpose was to learn more about technology rather than to garner instructional ideas. As one teacher described her experience:

> I acted as an escort for some visitors and showed them different classrooms . . . It was very interesting for me because this is the first time for me to see what others are doing in their classrooms and how they're using the computers. I think I'm going to suggest that maybe we do this occasionally to give the teachers some fresh ideas and to share and exchange knowledge.

Teachers also started to suggest sharing new techniques with their colleagues who were not directly involved in the project. For example, one teacher reported, "I realized after this conference that I need to share with the other math teachers what we are doing with the graphic calculator and to extend the program to more than the ACOT classes."

Team Teaching

Along with new instructional patterns that emerged during the invention stage came increased collaboration about instructional topics. The greatest degree of interaction occurred at sites that decided to formalize team-teaching arrangements, a decision that was made by the teachers themselves rather than imposed by district or school administrators. Given the differences in the contexts at each site, different team-teaching configurations evolved, varying along such dimensions as the number of team members, student grouping, interdisciplinary approaches, and grade-level assignments. As the benefits of team teaching became more apparent, ACOT staff encouraged this arrangement at all of the sites.

Team-Teaching Obstacles.   In the beginning, teachers frequently viewed team teaching as a lot of additional work for relatively little gain. Natural differences—in personalities, technical knowledge, teaching styles, grading policies, and approaches to discipline— became obstacles.

For some teams, personality differences created only minor problems as teachers came to know each other better. Other teams, however, found that personality problems carried over from year to year, becoming extremely divisive:

> I must say that the team-teaching approach seems to create some friction; jealousies seem to arise when one teacher thinks another teacher is doing something that makes him or her look good and the other teacher look bad. I think it is unfortunate. We should dismiss our personalities and subjective feelings about things and get on with teaching. If we let students and their learning come first, everything else would fall into place.

Differences in technical knowledge among teachers also led to conflicts and feelings of competition:

> As things become more competitive in terms of the use of equipment and software, and as some of us have become more competent, some of those who have been the "kings" have been

challenged and are reacting in unfortunate ways which is creating some tensions.

One site decided to have ongoing meetings for project teachers to air feelings that were building up among the teams. In the meetings, staff members were encouraged to be sensitive to one another, discussing issues and situations but avoiding personal attacks.

Teachers found it easy to agree in principle as they planned in teams. However, when they began teaching together, differences became more obvious. One such difference was teaching style. For example, in one team one teacher believed in allowing students enough time to finish an assignment, while the other teacher stuck to a predetermined schedule. Another team discovered they held divergent views about the structure of mathematics and their approaches to answering students' questions. One team teacher reported, "I'm also trying to impress on him that math is not just the calculating in the problems he gives. The thinking process of setting it up is math, too." Like many teachers, ACOT teachers felt strongly about their teaching philosophies and styles. Consequently, they were resistant to changing their own styles and at the same time hesitant about imposing their techniques on other teachers. Moreover, while some teachers enjoyed working closely with colleagues, others were reluctant to relinquish their autonomy:

> Moving from an independent teacher to a team teacher without much preparation contributed a great deal to my feelings of aimlessness and lack of control. It worked, but I was uncomfortable with it. I feel better about being in charge of teaching and the curriculum.

Some teachers found that they were defining their team teaching roles differently. For example, one teacher felt it was appropriate to work on individual projects or to leave the room when the other person was "teaching." The other teacher, feeling that a team approach involved more than a simple division of responsibilities, commented, "Those opportunities to fit things together don't come up unless you're right there in the classroom paying attention. He feels if I'm teaching there's no need for him to be there."

Inevitable differences in discipline and grading policies created initial obstacles to team teaching. Some teachers believed in making computerized summaries of scores and grades available to students,

while others felt that such a policy created competition and emphasized grades over substantive learning. Teachers also expressed
frustration over their varying approaches to classroom management
and discipline:

> I don't believe that Ana's standards of discipline were the same as
> mine. She was very patient with the children and didn't use
> discipline techniques. Their behavior tended to get out of hand
> before she brought them back, which frustrated me.

Team teaching also required planning time during the school
day—an expensive, and at some sites unrealistic, requirement. In
addition, physical settings sometimes hindered the opportunity for
spontaneous interaction and cooperative planning among teachers.
While some teams were able to overcome the obstacles inherent in
team teaching, others eventually reduced the amount of team teaching or dropped the arrangement altogether. The words of one teacher
who discontinued team teaching reveal the desire for autonomy:

> I really feel better about being solely in charge of my own classes.
> Now when I come in at off-hours to work, I know that I'm working
> for myself. You just don't feel the same when it's a team. I need to
> feel that student performance results directly from my teaching.

Advantages of Team Teaching.   The sites that continued with
team teaching found various ways to overcome the obstacles.
Proximity between classrooms and offices facilitated greater contact
among teachers. Regularly scheduled time for meetings during the
school day further enhanced the process of cooperative planning. As
described by one teacher, common planning time was a critical support:

> The fact that Ellen and I can sit down, coordinate lessons, and
> get a chance to talk is a very important thing to what it is we are
> trying to do out here. I need to campaign that all teachers should
> have time to coordinate with a team teacher [because of how
> important it is] to the learning process.

Teachers also became more proficient at using available time.
They learned how to interact with each other and how to prioritize
and accomplish tasks during their planning time. Some of the most
important tasks were setting goals and blocking out lessons so that

both team members understood what needed to be done. Having time to plan reduced stress and eased tensions about "not knowing what direction we were going." In the words of one teacher:

> As far as the team, what we expect from one another, it's so much more clear. Just getting to know each other, what they consider important, has really helped make this a very workable situation. I look back at my first year when I really wasn't sure about what was expected of me and how to function.

Successful teams also resolved personality differences and reached consensus about individual teaching styles, discipline policies, and the definition of team teaching. A coordinator described an effective teaching team at her site:

> Rob and Ilene are our experts and certainly role models for any study on how team teaching can and should be done . . . They strive to avoid the pitfall of thinking maybe they can get a few papers graded or write up a test or any of the other hundreds of things they could be doing while the other teacher is "on." The first priority for the time the other teacher is leading the discussion is to support that person. Nothing else takes precedence.

In addition, successful teams managed to reduce competition among teachers, learning to draw upon one another's areas of expertise and specialized knowledge. Although problems reappeared periodically over the years, the benefits outweighed the obstacles, leading the teachers to stick with the teaming approach.

Those ACOT teachers who continued with team teaching began to reap the rewards of collaboration. They developed a strong camaraderie and gleaned support from one another. The joint planning sparked ideas among teachers and increased their enthusiasm. At team meetings, teachers discovered ways to connect and improve upon activities and strategies they had tried individually. In addition, the discussions led to the development of new methods and became a powerful way of lesson planning. Moreover, the team approach allowed teachers to plan activities based on the strengths of each team member. Teachers found that their varying approaches could be complementary and benefit rather than hinder student learning. For instance, one teacher reported, "Lois was telling me that she was really impressed with the different way I covered the use of the trig functions today and how well that complemented what she had done. She thought the kids would come away with a better understanding."

The team approach also allowed teachers to provide more individual help and gave them more flexibility in grouping students. For example, one team decided to have one teacher take small groups to the biology lab while the other remained in the classroom. This decreased the amount of lab equipment needed and made it easier to monitor students and answer questions. Other teachers tried a similar strategy with a chemistry class. Even within the classroom, teachers could work with smaller groups requiring help in particular areas. In addition, teachers could vary their teaching assignments with small groups:

> I am pleased with the way Algebra 1 has turned out. We have the students working in two groups, and Jean and I switched groups this week. She was getting frustrated with the group she had that just didn't follow through. So it was a good idea just to shift to keep from getting burned out on one group. This wouldn't have happened in a regular classroom.

The teachers also reported that teaming increased what teachers were able to accomplish during a class period and made it easier to spot patterns of student misunderstanding.

When a team member was absent, the instructional program continued on schedule. One teacher commented, "Classes just go on whether we have a teacher here or a substitute. It's really working great in terms of the team knowing what others are doing and being able to cover when somebody is out." Without the concern over the progress of their classes during absences, teachers felt more comfortable about attending professional conferences or training scheduled during the school year.

Interdisciplinary Teaching. The team-teaching arrangement allowed ACOT teachers to develop and implement interdisciplinary curriculum. Interdisciplinary teaching occurred across a variety of subject areas, such as math/science, life skills/English, and history/literature. Teachers also combined a number of subject areas into one class; for example, a class called Strategies included math computation, problem-solving, science, and health.

As teachers became involved in interdisciplinary teaching, they began to identify a number of benefits. Students started to understand the integration among subject areas instead of viewing them as separate, unrelated topics. For instance, a high school teacher noticed that "the students don't differentiate between math and science now. It is exciting to have an opportunity to work in an interdisciplinary way." Students exhibited greater interest in their work and started to ask questions indicating their integration of subject areas:

> In the course we are teaching—American literature and history together—the students are really putting the two together . . . It will help them learn two areas which in the past students thought were boring. Now they are thinking and asking questions about it.

In addition, teachers discovered that students in their team-taught classes could handle more advanced material than those in traditional classes. For instance, a mathematics teacher noticed "a great difference in the amount of understanding the ACOT students have as compared with the students in the two regular classes that do not have the luxury of the teaming approach." A math/science team found that they were teaching concepts that other science teachers avoided because they believed students couldn't do the math involved. The integration also helped math/science teams in their goal of helping students to develop problem solving skills in mathematics rather than simply seeking solutions.

Teachers noted an increase in their own enthusiasm and knowledge as they became involved in interdisciplinary teaching. Their abilities to mesh their curricula exceeded their initial expectations. At the secondary level, strong subject matter boundaries started to diminish, and teachers began to seek out instructional resources and opportunities in other subject areas. As one teacher phrased it, "Team teaching is interesting because I concentrate on math, but I try to think of the science applications of it. I look for more ideas and materials than I would as a solitary teacher."

At one site the team-teaching and interdisciplinary approach developed by ACOT teachers became a model for classes throughout the school and district. A principal at another high school in the district, highly impressed with the approach, located funding to modify the model and develop curriculum for use in other urban schools— even those without the same access to technology.

INSTRUCTIONAL CHANGE AND COLLEGIAL SHARING IN ACOT CLASSROOMS

In the ACOT project, changes in collegial sharing were closely linked with instructional innovation, each enhancing the other. In Chapter 3 we discussed new patterns of teaching and learning that emerged over time and described five stages of instructional evolution in the project classrooms. Figure 7.1 depicts the relationship between the instructional evolution and collegial sharing among teachers.

In the entry stage of the project, teachers demonstrated little penchant for significant instructional change, and their interactions were infrequent and focused on emotional support. In the adoption stage, teachers used technology to support traditional instructional and learning activities; collegial sharing increased but included primarily technical assistance. The adaptation stage brought changes in the efficiency of the instructional process, and the substance of their interactions included sharing of instructional strategies.

As teachers eventually reached the appropriation and invention stages, their roles shifted and new instructional patterns emerged.

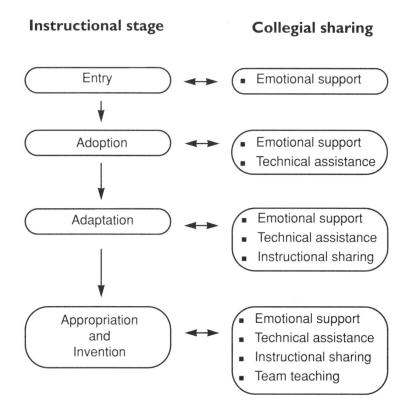

Figure 7.1 The relationship between instructional evolution and collegial sharing

Similarly, teachers collaborated more about instructional topics. At many sites increased collaboration led to team teaching. At first, teachers viewed team teaching as more demanding than beneficial. But as sites continued with team teaching and found ways to overcome the inherent obstacles, benefits began to emerge. Eventually, team teaching led to interdisciplinary teaching, which held additional advantages for both teachers and students. The list that follows summarizes the advantages of team teaching for the teachers:

- Shared responsibilities
- Increased camaraderie, enthusiasm, and support
- Development of activities based on teacher strengths
- Development of new ideas and teaching methods
- Use of approaches that promote student understanding
- Increased flexibility in grouping students
- Increased individual help for students
- Increased amount accomplished during class period
- Greater ease in identifying student misunderstanding
- Continuity of instructional program when one teacher is absent
- Development of an interdisciplinary curriculum
- Greater student ability to handle more advanced material

THE LINK BETWEEN TECHNOLOGICAL INNOVATION AND COLLEGIAL SHARING

In studying school change, researchers often investigate the adoption of innovations to determine what factors influence educational reform. Others examine barriers to and supports for collegial sharing and the impact of teacher interaction and collaboration on school effectiveness. This chapter linked these two distinct lines of research by illustrating the symbiotic relationship between innovation—in this case, the introduction of technology to the classroom—and collegial sharing among ACOT teachers as they worked together to adopt the innovation.

The Success and Failure of Innovation

Researchers investigating the success and failure of educational reforms have found that innovation can be extremely difficult to institutionalize because homeostatic forces in schools are more powerful than innovative forces (Joyce, 1982). In addition, teachers may resist change because the innovation comes from policymakers or nonteaching experts (Butt, 1984; Common, 1983), with little exchange between outsiders and practitioners about what curricular innovations mean in various classroom contexts (Swanson-Owens, 1985). Serious commitment from teachers occurs only after teachers use the new program or innovation and see that it really does assist them in teaching their students (Gersten & Guskey, 1985). However, these types of changes do not occur quickly, but evolve over a period of time (see Chapter 3). In addition to identifying time as a critical resource, researchers point to the importance of a supportive organizational environment and collegial sharing in moving teachers toward the adoption of innovations (Educational Technology Center, 1985; Henson, 1987; Joyce, 1982).

The Importance of Collegial Sharing

Although innovation can be supported by collegial sharing, the dominant pattern in schools continues to emphasize teacher autonomy rather than collaboration. For decades, the "cellular organization" of schools has persisted, where teachers expect to teach students without assistance from others and are assigned specific areas of responsibility (Lortie, 1975). The endurance of this pattern hinders attempts to create collaborative environments where teachers regularly talk with each other, observe one another, and reflect on their teaching. In school restructuring, teacher isolation has been identified as the most powerful impediment to reform (Lieberman, 1995).

In contrast, researchers identify regular opportunities for interaction with colleagues as important for a successful work environment (Purkey & Smith, 1983) and essential to creating professional school cultures (Lieberman, Saxl, & Miles, 1988; Miller, 1988). Little change will take place in schools unless teachers are observing, helping, and talking with each other (Barth, 1990). Teacher interaction in effective schools tends to be frequent, task focused, and widespread (Little, 1982; Rutter, Maughan, Mortimore, & Ouston, 1979). In many schools, however, opportunities for collaboration are limited and communication tends to be informal and infrequent, even though teachers believe their teaching could be improved by working with colleagues (Corcoran, 1988). In addition, teacher attitudes and workloads may inhibit interaction and collaboration (Sandholtz, 1989).

Attempts to increase collaboration frequently involve formalized restructuring efforts. Instructional arrangements are realigned so that teachers work together in various types of teams or units. In some cases, teams are organized across grade levels and across disciplines. These types of changes in school structures increase the incidence of collaborative teaching and the overall amount of task-related communication (Charters, 1980). Moreover, students in team-taught classes show better attitudes toward school (Cotton, 1982; Sigurdson, 1982), decreased discipline problems (Schmidt & Kane, 1984), and achievement gains (Costello, 1987; Schmidt & Kane, 1984; Sigurdson, 1982). However, teachers demonstrate reluctance to sustain team allegiance over time (Charters, 1980) and need long-term assistance to make teaming work effectively and efficiently (Rutherford, 1981). In addition, mandated teaming and collaboration can result in "contrived collegiality" that overrides rather than promotes teachers' professionalism (Hargreaves, 1994).

CREATING COLLABORATIVE ENVIRONMENTS

This chapter highlights three main issues relevant to educational innovation and teacher collaboration. First, similar to the findings of other researchers (Barth, 1990; Fullan, 1990), our results demonstrate that the adoption of innovation and the creation of a collaborative environment are complementary conditions for change. Individuals interested in school change err if they focus only on one of these conditions. Change occurs most quickly in environments where innovation and collegial sharing are operating simultaneously, each promoting the other. At each of the ACOT sites, the schools were already involved in some level of restructuring, as evidenced by their submission of proposals and their selection to participate in this innovative technology project. The schools' restructuring efforts aided the implementation of the ACOT project, and, conversely, the introduction of technology enhanced their restructuring endeavors. Similarly, case studies of schools that have been successful at restructuring indicate that breaking down teacher isolation and increasing opportunities for teachers to work together are critical factors in achieving other goals (Berry, 1995; Smylie & Tuermer, 1995; Whitford & Gaus, 1995).

Second, innovations involving technology can have a particularly potent effect on collegial sharing. Since training opportunities within districts are typically limited, and so few schools have on-site technical support available (Office of Technology Assessment, 1995), teachers often can only turn to each other when they need training or assistance with troubleshooting. Moreover, technology opens up additional ways for teachers to share across sites. For example, telecommunications networks allow asynchronous communication. Given the differing schedules of teachers—especially those in different schools, districts, and even states—being able to communicate without being in the same place at the same time is a boon. In addition, telecommunication permits long-distance communication and collaboration without teachers even leaving the classroom.

Third, collegial sharing is more likely to occur in schools when teachers have a personally meaningful reason for collaboration. At the ACOT sites, emotional support, instructional sharing, and collaboration increased because teachers sought each other's help in their attempts to adapt to their innovative classrooms. Rather than "contrived collegiality," interactions of ACOT teachers exhibited the characteristics of "collaborative cultures," where collaborative working relationships are spontaneous, voluntary, development oriented, pervasive across time and space, and unpredictable (Hargreaves, 1994). The innovative ACOT project legitimized teachers countering the norm of isolation that persists in schools. As with other types of school innovation (Smylie & Tuermer, 1995), collegial sharing increased ACOT teachers' willingness to experiment and take risks, and in this way promoted instructional change in their classrooms.

Recognizing the potential benefits of collegial sharing, ACOT developed a tool specifically designed to help teachers exchange ideas about integrating technology into instruction. The next chapter tells the story of one teacher who used this tool in a unit called "Journey Through the Twentieth Century."

8

Integrating Technology
into the Curriculum:
An Exemplary Unit
of Practice

❝ *I find myself sitting there as a coworker, and we can both look at the student's work, and make comments about it, and the students will often not feel as self-conscious about this piece of work as they would if they were working with a piece of paper or constructing something out of a piece of clay . . . That's one of the ways that I endeavor to teach, but with technology it's much easier to do.* ❞

After working alongside his students using technology, Dan Tate began to feel like a coworker, and his views about the potential of technology in the classroom shifted. When he initially joined the project, Mr. Tate wanted his students to learn the new technology that ACOT provided, but he wondered whether time spent learning the mechanics of the hardware and software would take time away from an already full curriculum. Before long, Mr. Tate realized that the most effective way to teach students to use technology was in the context of meaningful learning activities. This chapter tells the story of how Mr. Tate took a unit he considered one of his best, "Journey Through the Twentieth Century," and adapted it to include technology. Through the process, Mr. Tate recognized that when technology is integrated into the curriculum and not taught as a separate subject, concerns about curricular tradeoffs diminish and teaching and learning are enhanced.

Though not teaching in one of the original ACOT sites,[1] Mr. Tate joined the project in 1992 when ACOT began a partnership with the National Alliance for Restructuring Education. As one of the teachers involved in this partnership, he benefited from a support process specifically designed to help teachers implement and integrate technology into their classrooms. In this chapter, we first discuss the goals of the partnership, and we describe the support process ACOT developed, called the unit of practice (UOP). We next examine how Mr. Tate planned and implemented his specific unit of practice. Finally, we reflect on how the unit exemplified both technology integration and constructivist, project-based learning.

THE ACOT AND NATIONAL ALLIANCE PARTNERSHIP

In 1992 the National Alliance for Restructuring Education received funding from the New American Schools Development Corporation (NASDC) to create "break-the-mold" schools as part of a nationwide reform effort. The National Alliance, organized by the National Center on Education and the Economy (NCEE), included ACOT as one of its partners.

At the beginning of the ACOT project, ACOT staff allowed events to unfold and evolve (see Chapter 1). However, the nature and goals of the Alliance project required them to create specific interventions

---

1. Teachers described in previous chapters worked at one of the five original ACOT sites. Mr. Tate worked with ACOT during the 1992–1993 academic year.

supporting teacher and school change that could ultimately be used in other schools throughout the country. ACOT's goals were to help Alliance teachers successfully integrate technology into their classrooms and to help them move as rapidly as possible toward a more constructivist approach to teaching. Given the uncertainty about ongoing funding for the project, the Alliance hoped that the instructional evolution evident in ACOT classrooms (see Chapter 3) could be replicated at a much faster pace in Alliance schools.

ACOT equipped Alliance schools with a variety of technologies, but more importantly, it provided staff development and ongoing support for teachers. Like their counterparts in ACOT classrooms, Alliance teachers received technology training, professional release time, and access to an electronic network for sharing ideas and supporting each other. However, given the large number of teachers and classrooms involved in the project (12 Alliance schools in three states) and the small number of support staff available to work with the teachers, ACOT staff members realized that they would have to create new ways to provide ongoing, long-distance support.

The Unit-of-Practice Process

To this end, ACOT began implementing a support process called the unit of practice (UOP) with Alliance teachers.[2] Specifically created to help teachers integrate technology into the curriculum, the UOP is a tool designed to encourage teachers to experiment with, learn, and implement new teaching approaches. The unit of practice grew out of ACOT staff's desire to develop an instrument that could be used across all ACOT sites as an indicator of classroom change. Since it could easily be shared electronically among Alliance teachers, partners, and ACOT staff, it provided a relatively inexpensive and time-effective means of supporting teacher collaboration and instructional change. The UOP process also helped teachers develop a common language for reflecting on and sharing different components of a teaching episode, thereby facilitating collegial support. A unit of practice does not refer to a teaching unit in the traditional sense, nor is the process synonymous with lesson planning.

The UOP process can be applied to any learning project regardless of scope or scale. The process can involve a single task that is part of a larger lesson or a learning activity that extends over days, weeks, or months. To begin the UOP process, teachers select a teach-

2. The unit of practice was originally called the unit of study. Participants at the teacher development centers continue to use the UOP process.

ode that has been particularly successful in the past and then
bout how they might enhance or extend it using technology.
teachers focus on a teaching episode that has already been
nented, rather than having them develop an entirely new lesson,
ases teacher anxiety about risk taking and gives teachers a more
geable starting point for thinking about technology integration.
f technology is effectively integrated into the lesson and not sim-
dded on, teachers implementing the UOP process learn quickly
changing one component of a lesson—in this instance, adding a
technological tool—has ramifications for other components of
teaching episode. For example, the introduction of spreadsheet
tware to the study of graphing influences student tasks, lesson
ganization, and student assessment. The unit-of-practice process
ovides a way for teachers to envision the components of a prospec-
ve learning activity in one integrated whole. These interrelated
components include

- *Standards:* What objectives are set for learners? Why are they
  important? How do the objectives fit into overall district, state, or
  national frameworks?
- *Tasks:* What activities will students be doing? The nature of a task
  can be specified or open ended, it can be very simplistic or very
  complicated, and it can be concrete or abstract.
- *Interactions:* Who talks and works with whom? How will
  students and teachers work together? Who initiates interactions?
- *Tools:* What materials and equipment will be used to complete
  tasks? What tools will students and teachers use?
- *Situations:* Where will the activity take place? How long will
  students have to work on the activity?
- *Assessments:* What criteria will be used to evaluate student work?
  How do students, teachers, parents, and administrators know
  that learning standards are reached or exceeded?

Since these components are interrelated, the UOP process is
analogous to an ancient Chinese game, the tangram. In this game,
tiles of different shapes and sizes fit together to form a square.
However, the tiles can also be positioned to form a wide variety of
other shapes, such as a cat, a bird, a sailboat, or a house. The tiles
take on unique and specific characteristics, but only in relation to the
other pieces. No piece can be defined or fully understood except in
relation to the others. In this way, the UOP is like the tangram:
Teachers can address the components in any order, but a change in
any one component has potential to trigger change in the others.

The UOP process also helps teachers create a specific action plan for technology integration. Teachers using it think about each of these components in terms of how the teacher previously organized and conducted the teaching episode. From this starting point the conversation turns to the future: How would the teacher do things differently next time? Why? This comparison of past and future leads to defining action steps: What does the teacher have to do to get ready for the next time the lesson is implemented?

Although the UOP process can serve a variety of purposes, the primary intent for its use with the Alliance teachers was to provide a framework for discussion between teachers and ACOT staff. Ultimately, the goals for introducing the UOP were (1) to prompt teachers to confront their deeply held beliefs about teaching and learning, and ultimately their instructional practices, by starting a meaningful dialogue among educators and (2) to help teachers create specific, detailed plans for change that could be used in their own classrooms.

Starting a Meaningful Dialogue

After being trained to use the UOP process, Alliance teachers developed UOPs for use in their classrooms and sent them electronically to ACOT staff for feedback. ACOT staff members then met to brainstorm specific ideas for assisting teachers. They sent the UOP forms back to teachers with suggestions for improvement, and information on technological tools, software, and other resources that might be worth examining. Most feedback, however, took the form of questions to prompt their thinking: "Any thoughts of collaborating with other teachers?" "How will students be interacting?"

Once a dialogue began between teachers and ACOT staff members, teachers continued to exchange ideas using electronic mail. Alliance teachers also shared their UOPs with one another and with other Alliance partners. Ultimately, ACOT staff believed that the feedback provided by the unit-of-practice process would help teachers develop new ways of thinking about, talking about, and doing instruction.

AN EXEMPLARY UOP: "JOURNEY THROUGH THE TWENTIETH CENTURY"

The remainder of this chapter describes how the UOP process, as well as the introduction of technology to the classroom, influenced the beliefs and instructional practices of one Alliance teacher, Dan Tate. As he integrated technology into an existing unit called

● **Dan Sutch** Learning Researcher

1 Canons Road Harbourside
Bristol BS1 5UH United Kingdom
tel +44 (0)117 915 8221
fax +44 (0)117 915 8201
dan.sutch@futurelab.org.uk
www.futurelab.org.uk

"Journey Through the Twentieth Century," Mr. Tate changed the unit's standards, tasks, situations, interactions, and assessment—and ultimately changed his views about teaching and learning.

The Classroom Context

Mr. Tate, a sixth-grade teacher, had been teaching for six years before volunteering to participate in the Alliance project. His school, located in a middle-class rural community in the northeastern United States, enrolls approximately 250 students in grades K–12 and has two sixth-grade classes. Mr. Tate tries to work with the other sixth-grade teacher, Lucille Jackson, as much as possible but finds that "team teaching is difficult to schedule." For part of the day, students rotate through both sixth-grade classrooms. Mr. Tate typically focuses on mathematics and science, and Ms. Jackson teaches social studies and writing.

Unit Background: Mr. Tate's Starting Point

Mr. Tate was originally inspired to create "Journey Through the Twentieth Century" while on a field trip to visit a nearby marble sculptor who was designing the Korean War Memorial for display in Washington, D.C. Although the purpose of the field trip was to give his students "an appreciation of home," Mr. Tate came away from the experience with a new awareness of how little his students knew about major events in the 20th century, such as the Korean War:

> They knew where Korea was, but they really didn't know anything about the war . . . I just started popping questions at them about this century. Then I realized in eight years we're going to be looking back at the last one hundred. It's going to be a topic on the news. We're going to be trying to teach it. So what I decided to do was to have the kids just start exploring some of these events and cultural phenomena that happened in this century.

After this experience, Mr. Tate planned and taught a unit designed to expose students to societal changes in the 20th century. He considered it the best unit he had taught during the previous year.

Mr. Tate, who had only one low-end computer in his classroom when he originally implemented the unit, did not use technology extensively in his instruction. When the Alliance project began, ACOT donated new computers, video recorders, printers, and a liquid crystal display (LCD) panel to Mr. Tate's school. Mr. Tate received a high-end computer for his classroom, and he and his students shared

10 portable computers with three other classes in their building. If necessary, his class could borrow additional portable computers from teachers in the school's other buildings.

Anxious to see what he could do with the unit by using technology, Mr. Tate planned to experiment. Before beginning the unit, he claimed, "I'm going to try everything I can this year and see what works." Before he started experimenting, however, Mr. Tate received feedback from ACOT staff on his ideas as well as suggestions for improving the unit.

The Unit of Practice as a Process of Support

After developing an initial outline for the UOP, Mr. Tate shared his ideas over the course of several months via electronic mail with ACOT staff and other Alliance partners. ACOT staff encouraged him to describe the unit's learning outcomes and assessment strategies more thoroughly and recommended that students work in groups to research a specific decade rather than working individually on investigating a single year. They also suggested expanding the role of technology in the unit by using portable computers and video cameras for data collection and telecommunications to do a parallel study with students in another school. In addition, ACOT staff also began researching relevant laser discs and software programs that they thought might interest Mr. Tate.

Expanding the Unit with Technology

One software program recommended by ACOT influenced significantly the way Mr. Tate eventually implemented the unit. This software, which allows interactive data analysis, led Mr. Tate to reevaluate the unit's organization:

> Now I'm looking at this software as being the place that I should start this unit of practice by having the students do some research on social trends and patterns that . . . shaped the way people were thinking.

He envisioned, for example, how collecting data on leisure activities in the 1940s might eventually lead students to research the invention of television and its impact on social activities.

At first Mr. Tate wasn't exactly sure how he could best use this software within "Journey Through the Twentieth Century." Before starting the unit, he decided to give his students time to learn the program. Building on the ideas of another teacher within the Alliance project, Mr. Tate worked to create a lesson in which students would develop their own databases. Within a few months of his introduction to the software, Mr. Tate sent an electronic message to ACOT staff, sharing his excitement about what he and his students were doing:

> I knew when I first saw the software that students would fall in love with it as much as I did. But, I wasn't expecting this! . . . Two sixth-grade students put together a survey that they distributed to students in two classes. They then sat down with me to start putting the data into the database. What a breeze! . . . I only had to show them for about five minutes and then they were off.

Mr. Tate was impressed not only with how quickly these students caught on to the software but with how the technology promoted collaborative problem solving. Students worked together to figure out the intricacies of the software without extensive teacher guidance:

> As soon as the students had about four rows of data entered, they began to mess around with the Venn loops and axes. As they did so, they realized that some of the attributes they were entering weren't appearing in the loops. They investigated: "Let's check to see if it's in the database again. There it is, but it's spelled wrong." They began to realize that spelling was important but capitalization wasn't. I simply confirmed what they were discovering.

Mr. Tate also noticed how the software attracted other students in his class and how they taught each other how to use it. He observed, "I've seen no fewer than six other students entering information on the database, and I haven't been the one teaching them!" By the end of his students' introduction to the software, Mr. Tate felt convinced of its value for "Journey Through the Twentieth Century":

> I can't wait for tomorrow! Simply learning how to use this program has been a wonderful experience thus far. When we start using it as a tool for helping us analyze the social trends of the 20th century, there's no telling what may happen. Maybe nothing, but I have a feeling that these students are going to "push the envelope" on this one.

Unit Standards

The primary task of "Journey Through the Twentieth Century" required students to research major events and cultural phenomena of the century and then present their findings to peers and community members at an exhibition. In interviews, Mr. Tate suggested that when designing the unit he had more goals in mind for students than learning historical content knowledge.

In addition to helping students become "proficient with the equipment," Mr. Tate believed the unit would also help students learn "how to access information, how to understand information that someone else has written, how to interpret it and put it in your own words, where to find the information, [and] how to assemble the information into a story." Mr. Tate wanted students to learn how to access, use, and interpret information from a "vast assortment" of sources, including books from the library, interviews with local experts, historical artifacts, and technological resources such as laser discs and CD-ROM. He warned students that he expected much more than "an encyclopedia report," where students simply copy information from one source. He told them, "You're going to have to take this information and then decide what parts of it you are going to use. You can't just take one source of information and rewrite it."

After Mr. Tate decided to have students work together in groups during the unit, learning to cooperate became an important objective.

> I really wanted to stress [the] cooperative effort. I wanted the students to struggle with [it] somewhat, you know, and [learn] how to compromise with each other . . . I'm really trying to set the students up so they have to learn to cooperate in order to survive, in order to produce a final product.

Finally, Mr. Tate wanted this unit to strengthen the connection between his students and adults in the community. As students interviewed their parents, grandparents, and others who had lived through the events being researched, he hoped students would see that what they were learning had relevance outside of school.

Unit Implementation

"Journey Through the Twentieth Century" began in late March, when students received the first edition of the *Twentieth Century Times*, a one-page newsletter designed and written on the computer by Mr. Tate. The first edition contained two articles. Together, the articles gave a brief overview of the unit's goals and timeline and told students about the upcoming exhibition. Mr. Tate enjoyed using the newsletter format to keep students informed about the unit, and he hoped that it would motivate them. To create student interest, he adopted the persona of "Professor E. Ray Loomis, inventor of the world's first successful time machine," and asked questions such as, "Why are there hardly any houses built with front porches anymore?" And, "Are people any better off now that most everyone has an automobile?"

Mr. Tate and Ms. Jackson, the other sixth-grade teacher, divided their students into 10 teams of three or four students. They attempted to place within each group at least one student who was "very comfortable" with the technology as well as one student who could facilitate and motivate the group. Each group listed preferences about which decade to study.

On the first day of the unit, students also received a math assignment called "It's a Matter of Time." For the assignment, students constructed a chart that showed time travelers every possible combination of time units, from a second to a century, and the number of units in each combination. Mr. Tate thought of the assignment when students struggled during the previous week to figure out how many seconds are in a 10-hour period.

To ensure that each decade was represented, teachers made assignments based on students' preferences. Students then brainstormed together and completed a list of the types of events, trends, and phenomena they might like to research:

> I encouraged them, since it was brainstorming, to put down any ideas that came in their mind . . . Helicopters, if they're interested in helicopters, even if they weren't invented at that time, and then later they could cross it off their list.

While completing this task, students could use books in the classroom. A favorite was a 1,600-page resource encyclopedia that provided, for each month in the century, a summary statement of events, as well as photos and relevant articles.

Students then received a "Time Traveler's Itinerary" on which they scheduled the items they would be studying each day of the unit, for a total of 10 days. Mr. Tate required that students use the library, interviews, and artifacts for at least one of their topics, but they could determine other ways to locate information about their areas of interest.

As a group, the class discussed the available resources, such as books located in the classroom, the school library, and the regional library. Students could also obtain information from a local university via telecommunications or by putting messages on a computer bulletin board. Mr. Tate explained that he used the discussion of resources to help students narrow their research focus:

> Students are transferring the information from their brainstorming sheet onto another chart of places [where] they would [probably] look to find the information . . . I think that what they put down are things they would enjoy studying, but by doing this they can clearly see that some sources are going to be more available to them during the next few weeks . . . They are going to look back at their original brainstorming sheet and realize they can't do it all.

A few days into the unit, Mr. Tate was still struggling over how to use the interactive data analysis software introduced by ACOT staff to help students recognize historical trends and patterns. After looking through an almanac one evening, Mr. Tate thought that students could gather statistics—such as population, median income, or life expectancy—while doing their research and enter them into a database. He was worried, however, that students wouldn't be interested in these particular topics, so he decided to throw the question of how to use the software out to the students. In explaining this decision, he said, "I'll bring what I've put together and have the students look at it and begin thinking. I feel that the students are familiar enough with how the software operates and how the data can be used to prepare diagrams."

He was happily surprised when students generated numerous variables that interested them, such as average snowfall, high and low temperatures, speed records for cars, number of earthquakes, and death rate. He said, "I was really pleased with the results. I was worried last evening that there wouldn't be anything out there, but they proved me wrong."

Once students narrowed their research focus and determined where they would access information, Mr. Tate "turned them loose to work on their projects." After a visit to Mr. Tate's classroom during the second week of the unit, an ACOT staff member commented, "There were all kinds of activities going on at once, and if you were the type who wanted a very structured classroom, you would not have liked it. I mean, it was definitely freeform." Observers watched as Mr. Tate's students worked on a variety of tasks, both with and without the aid of technology. While some students used conventional resources such as books and magazines, others videotaped pictures from books to put into their projects, made video clips of movies from the 1930s, entered sports data into the interactive data analysis program, and used word processors to type up information. A girl investigating the turn of the century even phoned town hall from the classroom to get historical information on the town's buildings.

As part of the unit, Mr. Tate required students to conduct an interview as a means of data collection. He worked with the whole class to discuss who might be a good source of information, when the interviews could take place, and what types of questions the students might ask. Although many students relied on interviews with parents, grandparents, or family friends to complete this requirement, others went into the community to interview townspeople such as a retired schoolteacher who taught at the school in the 1960s or Vietnam veterans who were acquaintances of the school's bus driver. Students often used a video camera to tape their interviews with townspeople, and they took footage of the artifacts they saw. Many even took notes on portable computers.

During the last week of the unit, the class prepared for their exhibition, which would be open to the entire community. Working in groups, students created a general plan and sketch for their exhibit and determined which parts each person would contribute. The class discussed the types of artifacts that could be included, such as old photographs of relatives, old magazines, and even Perry Como records, and developed lists of artifacts they would have on display.

Mr. Tate and others deemed the exhibit a huge success. Virtually all of the students at the school viewed the displays at some point during the day, as did parents, administrators, former teachers, community members who had helped students collect information, and even the president of the state's Business Roundtable. Mr. Tate described the students' presentations as "grander" and "more professionally done" than those of the previous year. Many of them even surpassed Mr. Tate's expectations.

Students presented their work in a variety of ways, as these examples illustrate:

- The group studying the early 1900s created a 15-to-20-page magazine, complete with pictures they had imported on the computer. They built a newsstand for their display and offered samples of caramel corn they had made from an old recipe and

Moxie, a soft drink that predates Coca-Cola. One girl who researched women's suffrage had picket signs complete with slogans of that era.

- One student who worked in the group studying the 1940s was interested in learning about World War II. As part of his research, he interviewed an American who lived in Japan during that time. Much to Mr. Tate's surprise, Jeremy, described as rather "rough" by his teacher, showed up dressed in a kimono, and told about the war from the Japanese perspective, including a discussion of Hiroshima and Nagasaki.

- The group studying the 1930s had, according to Mr. Tate, the most "visually stunning" of the displays. They exhibited old movie placards and included video clips from old movies in the presentation. The students also dressed in the styles of the era.

During the exhibition, visiting students participated in a "trivia hunt." Each group wrote one or two questions that could be answered by looking at their displays or by talking with the presenters. Visitors who had the highest number of correct answers received a calendar published by Mr. Tate's students. The exhibition, which lasted all day, prompted a high level of interaction between students and visitors.

Student Assessment

Student assessment was an ongoing process during "Journey Through the Twentieth Century." Early in the unit, Mr. Tate emphasized the importance of using a variety of resources. Midway through the unit, he distributed a handout called "Assessment of Resource Usage" to make sure that students were "not just relying on encyclopedias, for example, or one particular interview" for all of their information. This sheet outlined the four-point standard by which students would be assessed; to reach the highest standard, students needed to use a variety of library resources, conduct an interview or survey of several individuals, and locate materials outside of school. Mr. Tate wasn't sure if the standard was reasonable, so he wanted to do an assessment early in the unit to make changes, if necessary:

> I don't know if I've made the standard high enough or low enough. I've asked that they use at least four different resources from the library and that they conduct at least one interview. We'll see if it's too low. I don't believe it's too high. I can collect the charts and assess them to this point . . . I can always place some additional factors into it, I suppose, if I find out that it's too low.

Mr. Tate also assessed student progress by meeting with individuals about their projects. He often met with students after school, to make sure they were on target, or looked "over their shoulders during study hall" to see what they were doing. Sometimes he caught problems early in the unit and could redirect students:

> I looked at his schedule . . . He had no less than 16 items he wanted to cover. I asked him how he planned to do this . . . He said that the other folks in the group were going to be able to help him because the were doing the same thing . . . They had a group meeting with me and I asked them if they understood my instructions . . . I explained to them what I expected them to do, and they decided that, yes, it was better if each one of them chose two or three things to concentrate on.

Other problems cropped up late in the unit:

> Upon receiving some of these final drafts, I immediately panicked because, frankly, what they handed to me was garbage. Yes, they had put them together using word processors . . . but as far as the actual writing itself, it had not been edited . . . I . . . told them it was unacceptable . . . I [emphasized] to them before they left school that they needed to produce final drafts that were to a standard we expected. They know what that standard is.

Several months after completing the unit, Mr. Tate commented on the standards he had set for the unit. Although the presentations exceeded his expectations in many ways, he still worried that he had set the standard about the number of sources too low. He found that students had used "8, 10, 12 or more" resources, when he had expected only 4. He realized, however, that for written reports, four sources of information at the sixth-grade level seemed about right. He agreed that perhaps their performance related more to a high level of student motivation than to standards being set too low.

REFLECTING ON THE UNIT AS A WHOLE

By implementing new technological tools in his classroom, Mr. Tate changed various components of the unit, such as standards, tasks, interactions, situations, and assessment. First, some of the unit's standards related specifically to technology: Mr. Tate wanted students to become proficient with the technology and to learn to access information from a variety of sources, including CD-ROMs and laser discs. Second, students completed many of their tasks—from doing research to producing the final exhibit—using computers, video recorders, and tool software such as word processing. Third, technology influenced the way students interacted with each other and with the teacher since students spontaneously taught what they had learned with the technology to their peers and to Mr. Tate. Fourth, Mr. Tate specifically extended the length of the unit to four weeks so that students would have more opportunities to use the new tools, thereby changing the situation in which students worked. Finally, Mr. Tate assessed student progress in part by how they used the new tools to access information.

The integration of technology into "Journey Through the Twentieth Century" also prompted Mr. Tate to use a more constructivist approach to teaching (see Chapter 1). His classroom became less teacher centered and didactic, and more learner centered and interactive. Although Mr. Tate used project-based, small-group instruction before the unit began, he also regularly engaged in whole-group, didactic instruction when he wanted to teach his students specific information. He explained:

> I think that I have been in some ways a fairly traditional teacher when it came to presenting information or giving instruction. I wanted them watching me, and I would instruct them on how to do something.

He found that this type of instruction did not work well, however, when students worked on the computers. Even if they all had their own computers on their desks and tried to follow along, he discovered that "you essentially need to be in 15 different places at once because there [are] going to be that many different questions."

In implementing the unit, Mr. Tate worked to change his role and that of his students. He stopped being the classroom expert and helped students see themselves as responsible for, and in control of, their own learning. He knew this wouldn't be an easy transition for some students. He explained:

> This is a first for them. They're used to my saying this is the kind of information they need to find, and this is where to find it. Now they're the ones identifying what the information is and identifying the resources as well, so it's going to be a challenge.

Although some students may have been reluctant to take more responsibility for their own learning during this unit, when it came to working with the technology, most quickly stepped into the role of expert. Mr. Tate was surprised both by how quickly the students came up with ideas for how to use the technology and by their willingness to share these discoveries with their peers. He even noticed them "sharing information at lunch." He also observed an increase in peer collaboration in his classroom and reported that students' desire to work together carried over to other classes as well:

> They're teaching each other a lot, and I don't think I've seen it to this extent in any other classroom. The students are really helping each other . . . and I've seen that carry over into other things . . . In math class, I see that so often, as opposed to the beginning of the year. Now when students are stuck, their peers will just as often say, "Let me help you. I won't give you the answer, but let me get you started."

Working side by side with his students while using the technology, Mr. Tate felt more like a coworker than an all-powerful, all-knowing teacher. He stated:

> Students and teachers have a markedly different relationship in the classroom setting when technology is used. The teacher becomes a coworker with the students as they each work on completing projects with the help of computers. Students tend to move ahead at a pace they're comfortable with. The teacher is no longer the provider of knowledge as students discover on their own.

Although technology made it easier for Mr. Tate to step into the role of classroom facilitator and implement a more constructivist teaching approach, he found nothing simple about designing and carrying out a project such as "Journey Through the Twentieth Century." Despite the support that he received from the Alliance, from ACOT, and from his school, it was challenging for him to coordinate student access to the different resources and technologies, and he stated that in the midst of the unit he sometimes felt like he had "a tiger by the tail." Well-designed constructivist projects such as this are energy intensive and cannot be implemented all of the time. While integrating technology into the curriculum is vital if these new tools are to become an effective educational resource, doing so is difficult and time consuming (Office of Technology Assessment, 1995).

Educational reformers advocate that teachers increase their use of technology and constructivist, project-based learning approaches. However, opportunities for teachers to learn to incorporate these strategies into their classrooms are not commonplace. The next chapter describes a staff development program specifically designed to introduce and support teachers as they begin using these instructional approaches in their classrooms.

9

Creating an Alternative Context for Teacher Learning

66 *This program is not about how to use equipment but rather a chance to explore how bringing this technology into the classroom will change teaching.* 99

As the case studies of Mrs. Bennett and Mrs. Lee illustrate, teachers usually begin using technology to replicate old patterns of instruction. It can be years before they progress to the stage in which they truly integrate technology and use these tools to their fullest potential. Movement toward technology integration and toward constructivist modes of teaching is often slow to nonexistent because staff development typically offered to teachers is inadequate. Frequently, teachers attend short workshops after school, are shown how to hook up and operate their equipment, and are then sent back into their classrooms with little or no follow-up support.

In 1991 a steering committee composed of ACOT staff, teachers, administrators, and researchers created a model of staff development that goes beyond the traditional in-service approaches so frequently used. The model is designed to help teachers from throughout the country, even those with significantly less access to technology than that found in ACOT classrooms, move through the process of change described in our evolutionary framework (see Chapter 3). Perhaps the most important objective of the project, however, is to prepare teams of teachers to return to their own schools as leaders, able to engage their colleagues with new ideas about learning and technology. Ultimately, the project's long-term goal is to create a network of schools, each prepared to offer this form of staff development to teachers from its own district as well as neighboring ones.

By design, ACOT's model of staff development is flexible, allowing schools and districts that implement the program to make modifications based upon site-specific strengths and constraints. Because of this flexibility, the model does not offer a specific "recipe" for teacher development that can simply be replicated, but rather a framework from which other schools and districts can build effective teacher development programs. According to the guiding principles of the model, which builds on years of ACOT experience in staff development as well as work by the Holmes Group (1990) and the Carnegie Forum on Education and the Economy (1986), effective staff development provides opportunities for teachers to

- observe and reflect on a variety of teaching strategies, including direct instruction, team teaching, collaborative learning, project-based learning, and interdisciplinary learning
- engage in hands-on use of computers, productivity software, camcorders, and telecommunications as tools to support learning through composition, collaboration, communication, and guided practice

- interact with students in real classrooms
- share knowledge and experience with colleagues
- create specific plans for technology use in their own classrooms and schools

This chapter describes the Teacher Development Center model and discusses visiting teachers' experiences as they participated in the program. Chapter 10 examines the center's impact on participants, the barriers that impeded participants' progress once they returned to their schools, and the supports necessary to sustain teacher change.

A NEW MODEL FOR TEACHER DEVELOPMENT

In 1992, ACOT, the National Science Foundation (NSF), and three school districts joined to create teacher development centers at three of ACOT's original sites.[1] At the centers, non-ACOT teachers spend time at the school site in which ACOT classrooms are located, observing and working in actual classrooms. ACOT calls this "situated teacher development" because the program is situated in a context of practice. Unlike typical after-school programs, this model of teacher development allows participants to see expert teachers modeling instructional practices as they work with students, thereby providing participants with a framework in which they can examine the results of these practices on student work and interactions.

The centers also differ from traditional forms of staff development because activities are learner centered and interactive. The design of this staff development model is based on the premise that adult learners, like children, should be given opportunities to construct and interpret meaning for themselves, rather than being fed information. The program's constructivist design models the types of learning environments implemented in ACOT classrooms.

The Teacher Development Center project has three major components: weeklong practicums during the school year, four-week summer institutes, and sustained support from project staff for visiting teachers once they have returned to their schools. Teachers who visit the centers can attend a practicum, a summer institute, or both

---

1. Although NSF funding ended in 1995, the three districts are continuing to operate the centers.

program components. Practicums are held at the ACOT sites over the course of the academic year during regular school hours. Summer institutes are also held at the ACOT sites, in conjunction with technology-enrichment programs for students. Each practicum typically accommodates 4 teachers simultaneously, while 24 teachers attend each summer institute. A coordinator at each center is responsible for implementing the program with the assistance of the ACOT teachers. Program coordinators also provide follow-up support for participants for one year after visiting the centers.

The curriculum at each center is flexible and differs from week to week and from site to site, depending on participants' interests and skills. As part of this flexible curriculum, participants at each center learn about integrating specific hardware and software into their instruction and explore issues such as interdisciplinary instruction, alternative assessment, project-based teaching, and team teaching. Participants spend much of their time at the centers observing in ACOT classrooms and working in learning teams with ACOT students. Teachers who attend either the practicums or summer institutes are required to plan technology-related projects for use when they return to their own classrooms.

The practicum and summer institute offer different types of experiences for participants. Part of this difference relates simply to the duration of the training: 5 days for the practicum and 20 days for the summer institute. Coordinators typically plan the practicums as an overview or introduction to a wide variety of topics. Participants have described the practicum experience as "a smorgasbord" where they leave "knowing a little bit about a lot of things" rather than having mastery over particular technology tools or teaching strategies, as they might when they complete the summer institute.

In addition to the duration, the practicum and summer institute experiences differ in other ways, giving each program component distinct advantages. At the practicum, participants observe and work in ACOT classrooms during the academic year. Class sizes are realistic, there is a curriculum to cover, and student learning must be assessed. In contrast, the summer institute offers "the best of all worlds." Class sizes are small, there are no curriculum mandates, and there are no standardized tests for students or teachers to worry about. While the summer institute gives teachers the chance to work side by side with students, to take risks, and to explore in a non-threatening environment, the practicum allows them to see the possibilities in a context that is similar to their own classrooms, making what they learned easier to transfer to their own situations.

PROGRAM PARTICIPANTS

During the first year, all participants who attended the Teacher Development Center project came from the districts in which the centers are located. Because demand for the program exceeded the number of teachers who could be accommodated, program coordinators and district administrators developed strategies to determine who would participate. One district selected participants by lottery. Principals from each school chose one team to apply for admission to the program. Administrators understood that if one team member decided not to attend the program, a new partner would have to be found or the team could not participate. At another site, the program coordinator designed a selection process with the assistance of the ACOT staff. Three staff members rated applications blindly and assigned points based on teachers' creative use of the technology already available at their schools. Teachers who scored over 75 points on their applications received further consideration. After conversing with these applicants' principals, the coordinator made the final selection of participants.

Since the school districts had to cover costs of substitute teachers for program participants, district administrators and principals gave significant input regarding who should attend the program. At times, concerns about fairness and equity led to conflicts within districts about who was selected to participate (see Chapter 10).

In the project's second year, attendance was open to districts throughout the country. Over 600 teachers—representing 30 districts, 15 states, and two foreign countries—participated in the program during its first three years of operation. When participants came from outside the districts in which ACOT sites are located, their home districts paid for substitute teachers as well as room, board, and travel expenses. In addition, each team of teachers paid a small fee to cover course materials.

Participants represented a variety of grade levels and disciplines, and included teachers in special education, Chapter 1, and bilingual education as well as administrators, resource personnel, and librarians. Participants' teaching experience ranged from 1 to 30 years, and their technological knowledge and expertise varied as well. Although some teachers had never used a computer before, others rated their proficiency with technology as "high" when compared with other educators in their schools. Most reported that they had never used, or were just beginning to learn, more sophisticated uses of technology such as multimedia, telecommunications, and spreadsheets.

To be accepted into the Teacher Development Center program, each teacher needed access to a computer, printer, and software in his or her classroom. This prerequisite was included in the project because teachers typically use technology more frequently if equipment is in their classrooms rather than in labs. The program also required teachers to attend in teams of two to four so that they could support one another when returning to their schools. Each two-teacher summer institute team received a computer from Apple Computer for completing the program. Some districts also provided a computer for each team. The combination of Apple and district support gave many teachers at least one computer to use in their classrooms.

ACOT staff strongly encouraged principals to attend selected portions of the program with their teams. Principals also made a commitment to support teachers in three important ways when the teams returned to their schools: (1) to provide time for teachers to plan together and to reflect on their practice, (2) to give recognition for the team's efforts, and (3) to ensure that teachers had the authority and flexibility to adjust daily instructional schedules and to develop curriculum objectives that promote team teaching and interdisciplinary instruction. ACOT staff included these components in the design of the project because they felt that principals' commitment to and involvement in a changing vision of learning and instruction were critically important to the success of the program.

TEACHERS' EXPERIENCES AT THE TEACHER DEVELOPMENT CENTERS

By studying these teachers' experiences, we learned that principles for creating successful learning environments for children apply to teachers as well. When teachers are learning to integrate technology into their classrooms, the most important staff-development features include opportunities to explore, reflect, collaborate with peers, work on authentic learning tasks, and engage in hands-on, active learning. All of these features characterize a constructivist learning environment. Teachers also appreciated receiving assistance in applying what they learned at the centers to their own classrooms and schools. The remainder of this chapter describes teachers' reactions to these program components.

The Value of a Constructivist Learning Environment

Teachers at each center had opportunities to construct their own knowledge about specific technological tools as well as technology integration. Although there was some didactic instruction on hardware and software, teachers usually "learned by doing" while the coordinator and ACOT teachers served as facilitators.

Compared with traditional classrooms, constructivist learning environments place more responsibility on students for their own learning. This type of responsibility can cause some children to feel frustrated and uncomfortable, particularly if they are accustomed to having a teacher who "transmits knowledge" to them. However, with this added responsibility comes freedom for individual exploration, hands-on practice, and reflection. Typically, once students overcome their initial discomfort, they begin to see the value of constructivist learning. From monitoring teachers' reactions to the program, we learned that adult learners are much like their young counterparts in their attitudes toward constructivist learning.

When teachers first arrived in project classrooms, they often felt overwhelmed, and sometimes frustrated, by the constructivist nature of the teacher development center experience. Teachers expected the typical in-service experience—a highly structured, didactic training session, where a trainer dispenses information. Instead, they faced a loosely structured, learner-centered model with time to explore, experiment, and discover on their own. Some teachers had a difficult time adjusting to this type of learning environment. Faced with learning a vast assortment of new skills in a relatively short period of time, many teachers at first believed that having the coordinator lecture would be the most efficient teaching approach.

Despite this initial reaction, most teachers soon adapted to the center's learning environment. Within a few days, teachers who had originally begged the coordinators for more didactic instruction began enjoying opportunities for exploration and discovery. For example, one teacher had the following before-and-after reactions:

> BEFORE: I can see the value of learning on the job; yes, we do learn more thoroughly, but it is also much more painful . . . This frustration does not lead me to want to discover more, but leads me directly to quitting and letting someone who does know what they are doing do it . . . I need more directions . . .

AFTER: This is a fabulous experience and certainly well worth it, whether you are a novice or a "tried and true." We "old timers" need these boosts to keep teaching fresh and exciting!

Many teachers commented on the differences between traditional in-service training and the teacher development center. For instance, one teacher said, "This training is different. How? In every way—philosophy, structure, technology, and content." Another commented:

> Isn't it interesting that the activities that work with kids are just as powerful with adult learners. For such a long time all in-services espoused cooperative learning, writing, discussion, etc., but they didn't model those strategies during the in-service. It's wonderful that we are finally getting beyond the telling and are into the showing and modeling when we talk about teacher training.

Time for Exploration and Active Learning. Like children, most teachers enjoy hands-on exploration. Although lecturing is the time-honored technique for covering the greatest amount of information, teachers, like students, quickly tire of being passive listeners. At the centers, teachers delighted in the chance to experiment and explore with technology. When asked to describe the most helpful or rewarding aspects of the practicum, teachers responded with comments such as this:

> To be honest, I was expecting to be extremely bored this week. All the in-services I have attended in the past have been informative yet not hands-on enough. Today has been wonderful. I feel like I have already doubled or tripled my knowledge of computers in one session because I actually got to touch and play with them.

The teachers' need for active learning became evident in their reactions to a three-day workshop conducted by outside trainers. At one site, the presenter used an approach that complemented the constructivist learning model at the teacher development center. Much of the training involved teachers and students working together in groups to explore the software and problem-solve on their own, with the presenter acting as a facilitator. Teachers' responded overwhelmingly favorably to the training. However, at another site, the trainer employed a completely different approach. Teachers sat through lectures for long periods of time and never had the chance to use the software with students. These teachers made extremely negative comments about the workshop. As one teacher explained, the presenter served as a "good negative role model for what not to do."

Time for Reflection.   Another important aspect of a constructivist environment is the emphasis on quality of understanding as opposed to quantity. Learners are actively engaged in constructing their own knowledge and in understanding rather than passively memorizing facts. In such an environment, learners have time to reflect on what they are learning rather than racing ahead in an effort to memorize even more information.

Although teachers wanted to learn all they could during the one- or four-week period at the teacher development centers, they quickly complained of overload if not given adequate time to think about the information they were processing. Attempts to rush through a set curriculum can often backfire with teachers, just as it can with students. At the centers, teachers highly valued time for reflection, either in a group discussion or when writing in personal journals. As one teacher recorded:

> Our reflection times have provided me the opportunity to share my fears, frustrations, questions, and excitement with others who understand where I am coming from.

The Value of Situated Staff Development

Learning is more meaningful when learners engage in activities that are directly related to their own needs. By working in real classrooms with real students, teachers are better able to see how what they are learning can be useful in their own classrooms. Staff development situated within the context of practice also allows participants to observe accomplished project teachers modeling a variety of teaching strategies, including the use of technology in project-based, interdisciplinary instruction. Observations gave some teachers new ideas for how they might integrate technology in their own teaching. For those participants who witnessed project teachers employing teaching strategies that they already used in their own classrooms, observations served as a source of validation. Observations also stimulated discussions about the program's philosophy and provided firsthand views of how technology can serve as a catalyst for change. We learned that opportunities to observe are most valuable when the coordinators act as guides and translators, through focusing observations and using them as a basis for discussion.

Classroom Observations. During the practicum, teachers had designated time periods to wander from classroom to classroom at their discretion. To take advantage of special lessons or activities, unscheduled observations also occurred from time to time. As one teacher explained, the participants could "drop everything and go into a classroom when they heard something exciting was going on." If teachers had questions about what they were seeing, they wrote them down rather than interrupting the flow of the lesson.

Because each teacher development center consists of real teachers in real classrooms, visitors did not always see perfect lessons in which teachers used strikingly innovative teaching strategies. In some instances, students appeared off task or the teacher seemed to be improvising. In addition, they saw ACOT teachers abandoning plans to use technology when equipment wouldn't work. Visiting teachers seemed surprised when ACOT teachers had trouble with equipment, thinking that they were "technology gurus" who could fix anything.

In addition, since ACOT teachers were in different stages of change (see Chapters 2 and 3), participants observed some teachers struggling with classroom management issues in the entry stage and others, in the appropriation stage, effectively integrating technology into their classrooms. Moreover, because ACOT teachers are encouraged to strike a balance between instructionist and constructivist activities, participating teachers sometimes observed traditional approaches such as direct instruction or lecture in ACOT classrooms. Some participants had expected technology to be used virtually all the time, when in reality a variety of instructional approaches are used.

Whether the observed lesson was an exemplar of constructivism and technology integration or something completely different, observations served as an important impetus for discussion among participants. During the first day or two at the centers, teachers often felt reluctant to evaluate and question what they had observed in project classrooms or to openly discuss and reflect upon their personal beliefs about teaching. Rather, they preferred to talk about surface-level features of project classrooms, such as hardware or software. As they spent more time at the centers, however, a level of trust emerged among participants and coordinators that allowed more open discussion of topics such as teaching philosophies, alternative assessment, technology as an instructional tool, and shifting student and teacher roles. Most participants valued discussing educational issues with their colleagues, as this excerpt illustrates:

> Having the time to talk with partners and colleagues is extremely important for support and validation. I certainly hope that our principal will allow my partner and me to have the opportunity to meet with each other, and with others on the staff, to plan.

A few teachers did not find classroom observations helpful, because they could not see anything beyond the extensive technology available in the ACOT classrooms. Some participating teachers started counting computers as soon as they entered the rooms, and then shook their heads in apparent disbelief. These teachers believed that what they observed at the teacher development center would not be applicable to their situations because they had only a few computers in their classrooms. For instance, one teacher commented:

> I learned I'd die for one computer for every team of four kids. I'd probably do similar types of instruction if I had computers available. Their applications were wonderful, but not very transferable.

In response to these types of feelings, the coordinators urged teachers to consider how they could make changes using the equipment they already had; reminded them to focus on constructivist teaching, not just on the use of technology; and offered suggestions on how to obtain additional resources.

The vast majority of participating teachers felt that observing in ACOT classrooms was one of the most valuable aspects of their visit to the center. For some teachers, simply watching how students used technology was eye-opening. For example, one veteran teacher who had been using a computer in his class for years was surprised to find out that "the ACOT teachers let the children operate the computers relating to their lessons." Similarly, another teacher commented:

> I was using computers before, but as a result of my experiences at the center, I am now allowing my children to have more control of the equipment. Before, I would have the children type on the word processor, and I would save it for them. Then in the evening I would print their things for them. Now I let them do it all.

Other teachers came away with specific ideas on integrating technology into instruction. One teacher commented that she had learned how to teach a computer lesson to a whole class and how to group children at computers. Another teacher stated, "I was really impressed with the way Mrs. James handled all the activities in the room. I am interested in learning how to plan, implement, and manage stations . . . It was so smooth in her classroom."

By observing technology use in different grade levels and subject areas—as well as for various instructional purposes—teachers acquired a vision of what was possible. Without this vision, teachers might have returned to their classrooms and simply used preexisting software for drill and practice. Many teachers also left with a better understanding of how constructivist learning environments change students' and teachers' roles and how technology can serve as a catalyst for this change. For instance, one teacher pointed out:

> ACOT teachers are attending to at least four things at once. They are not standing in front of the classroom trying to get all 30 students to pay attention to them. They are guiding students individually. They are very flexible.

Another teacher commented:

> I saw a variety of teaching styles within the ACOT classrooms. All seemed to benefit by having technology available to students. And in all styles, student collaboration and tutoring seemed accelerated by technology. Teacher as "expert" is forced to diminish since none has knowledge about all technology.

Working with Students.   Although participating teachers enjoyed *observing* ACOT students, actually *working* with students as they used the technology caused frustration and concern for some teachers. During summer institutes, for example, small groups of students teamed up with participating teachers to work on various projects. At one site, each teacher-student learning team had three days in which to create a presentation related to the overall theme of cycles. With the ACOT teacher serving as a resource, each learning team formulated a plan, decided how to integrate the available technology, and made a presentation at the end of the week.

When working in learning teams with students, participants worried that they would be unable to teach students, given their inexperience with new technological tools. Their concerns abated when they discovered that working with students allowed them to model problem-solving skills as well as practice new skills with the technology. Teachers also discovered how much they could learn about technology from students.

Seeing students in a new light, many teachers found it useful to learn firsthand what students are capable of doing when given the chance. Teachers admitted that before visiting the center they often underestimated students' capabilities. As one teacher noted:

> I had already been into the discovery learning type of teaching, but I still thought that I had to sort of keep control and do things for the children, but I found out that they were really able to do much more for themselves than I gave them credit for.

During summer institutes, teachers also worked with children who came to the program with little or no background in technology. In doing so, teachers saw how quickly even young students can learn relatively complex hypermedia applications or software programs. This experience gave teachers confidence that they, too, could teach students how to use technology, even when students were starting at "ground zero."

In some cases, teachers who were complete novices in using technology worried because they did not know more than their students. Their concerns mirrored those expressed by ACOT teachers in the first years of the project (see Chapter 5). In other instances, teachers learned about a technological tool only hours before being expected to teach students how to use it. In these cases, teachers voiced complaints such as this: "I wish I had more time to spend playing with my computer before the students came, so that I had a chance to try things before having to work with them." In some cases, teachers had trouble relinquishing control as they tried to step into the role of facilitator: "When working with students, I also have difficulty keeping my hands off the mouse; however, I am making a conscious effort not to help students unless they ask and definitely not to touch the mouse."

With encouragement from coordinators, most teachers gradually overcame their concerns about learning side by side with students. They often commented that the creation of teacher-student learning teams had distinct advantages over traditional staff-development opportunities. For example, while working in learning teams with students, teachers could model problem-solving skills:

> I enjoy learning and facilitating someone else's learning simultaneously. I think this is the ultimate way to teach because . . . teachers can develop the student's critical thinking by modeling, analyzing, and evaluating the problem-solving process as a team of learners. We are . . . participating as learners and teachers.

A risk-averse teacher noted:

> This experience has even made me take risks. I've decided the worst that can happen is I make mistakes and I need to ask others for help. I think if I show that I take risks and make mistakes in teaching, my children will feel more comfortable doing the same in learning.

Moreover, teachers found that working with students reinforced their own burgeoning technology skills. Instead of having to wait until they returned to their own classrooms in the fall, teachers could try out their newfound skills immediately. As one teacher commented:

> I taught a small group of second-graders a hypermedia application right after I learned the program. This was super, since it really made the program sink in for me . . . This was a great experience for me since I got to instantly use the information I was learning with students, so I got to practice how to teach these great things.

The Value of Specific Plans for Change

To structure their observations and transfer new ideas into their own classrooms, teachers planned projects to implement upon returning to their schools. Both practicum and summer-institute teachers developed formal, written proposals about how they would integrate technology into their instruction. Coordinators, and sometimes ACOT teachers, worked closely with participants to brainstorm ideas for projects and give guidance.

Teachers' plans varied tremendously in scope and focus. Some teachers planned small lessons, while others planned monthlong interdisciplinary, project-based units. Some teachers worked alone, while others worked in teams that crossed interdisciplinary, grade level, and school lines. For instance, an elementary teacher planned an interdisciplinary six-week unit called "Holidays Around the World." In this unit, students research and write a report on the country of their heritage, including information about the country's geography, climate, life forms, and culture. Students use a hypermedia application and a scanner to create the report, which is presented to the class using a television monitor or liquid crystal display panel. On the last day of the unit, students prepare a dish traditionally served on a holiday in their selected country.

While ACOT staff encouraged teachers to be ambitious and creative, they also urged them to be realistic and take into account the constraints of their settings, such as curricular mandates, lack of time, or lack of equipment. The major purpose of the project was to help teachers take the first step toward technology integration and constructivist teaching, using the resources they already had on hand. Through the process of planning their projects, even teachers with a minimum amount of technology realized that they did not need the same resources as ACOT teachers to make positive changes in their classrooms. As one teacher stated, "[I learned that] one computer can be an effective teaching tool in the classroom."

THE NEED FOR NEW FORMS OF STAFF DEVELOPMENT

To fully exploit the power of technology, teachers need adequate training and support. However, some reports suggest that only one-third of all K–12 teachers have had even 10 hours of computer training and that, on the average, districts devote no more than 15% of technology budgets to teacher training (Office of Technology Assessment, 1988, 1995). Even with more time and resources for technology training, current methods of professional development are woefully inadequate because most focus on learning about computers rather than on learning how to integrate computers into the curriculum. As such, these training programs do little but preserve the instructional status quo. Teachers condemn this type of staff development; they want "challenging experiences and opportunities to collaborate seriously with their peers who have good ideas and are excited about what they are doing" (Lewis, 1994, p. 508).

New forms of professional development need to be created that show teachers how to use technology to its fullest potential. The model designed and implemented by the Teacher Development Center project suggests that principles of instruction that are successful for young learners also apply to adults. Teachers who participated in the program benefited from hands-on, active learning; working with colleagues; reflection; and creating projects that could be used in their own classrooms. Perhaps most important, the Teacher Development Center project provided opportunities for teachers to work in real classrooms and to see models of constructivist teaching firsthand. The next chapter discusses the impact of these experiences on participants as they returned to their schools and describes the contextual barriers and supports that influenced them.

10

Back to the Real World: Opportunities and Obstacles in Staff Development

❝ *I look at my computer, and all it is is a glorified typewriter right now.* ❞

❝ *I never knew that technology would be something that would be so vital that I would be so interested in it and see how important it would be . . . It was just like a life-altering thing.* ❞

The two teachers just quoted attended the Teacher Development Center project and returned to their schools with drastically different outlooks about their future use of technology. School and district contexts influenced the extent to which teachers returning from the teacher development centers integrated technology into their classrooms. In this chapter, we describe the barriers teachers encountered and identify the potential impact of staff development when teachers can successfully overcome them. We also examine the types of supports school and district administrators can give to assist teachers as they work to change their instructional approaches.

BARRIERS TO CHANGE

Although most participating teachers left the teacher development centers hoping to integrate technology into their classrooms, they encountered barriers upon returning to their schools. Consistent with findings from other technology-related projects (Office of Technology Assessment, 1995), problems with access, lack of technical support, and insufficient time slowed teachers' progress and limited their abilities to share what they had learned with colleagues.

Limited Access

Although all participants had access to technology when they returned to their schools, many teachers complained that insufficient amounts of hardware and software impeded their progress. Coordinators tried to show participants how to successfully use only one or two computers, but after seeing what could be accomplished in technology-rich classrooms, participants often felt limited by and dissatisfied with their access to technology.

Some principals believed that teachers could more effectively use their limited technology by trying creative instructional approaches. One principal analyzed the problem as not a lack of technology but rather "a certain mentality that says everyone needs to be doing the same thing at the same time." Indeed, teachers who adopted a station approach—where groups of students rotate through a variety of different activities on a daily or weekly basis—discovered that they often could manage effectively with only one or two computers. Nevertheless, even teachers who used stations wanted more technology.

Limited access also affected participants' abilities to share their knowledge with colleagues. When teachers knew it was unlikely that they would be given their own equipment to use, they seemed less interested in learning about technology. As one principal commented, "It's hard to get teachers interested when they know there isn't money." One participant who successfully attracted her peers' interest in technology pointed out that concerns about access and training go together. Since her school received a large technology grant and planned to acquire new equipment, teachers wanted to learn from her. She stated, "Without the grant, the training would fall flat."

Equity is another issue that concerned participating teachers. While craving greater access, teachers stated that they did not want their peers or their principals to see them as greedy. Without enough computers to go around, the faculty sometimes became fragmented and competitive. As one teacher commented, "If we could all have a computer in every teacher's classroom, I think we would see no more competition, and 'Hey, have you seen this program!' would be more common." Rather than risk provoking jealousy, participants sometimes kept quiet about what they were doing in their classrooms and did not protest when equipment they could have used was given to other teachers.

Technical Problems

Unlike the ACOT teachers, most participating teachers did not have on-site technical support and found that technical difficulties impeded their abilities to implement what they had learned at the centers. Sometimes problems resulted from participants' lack of basic knowledge, while other times equipment simply malfunctioned. Whatever the cause, teachers frequently abandoned plans when they could not obtain technical support.

Many teachers lacked troubleshooting skills, and few had access to manuals that might have enabled them to solve their own problems. And, when equipment had to be sent out for repair, it sometimes was not returned for months. Although some participants managed to get help, teachers often became discouraged when their plans were delayed because the technology would not work. In a few cases, teachers' feelings of self-efficacy quickly diminished, making it less likely that they would continue using technology.

Teachers who did have basic troubleshooting skills found themselves in a different type of bind. Once word got around that a person knew how to troubleshoot, he or she was frequently called upon to fix other people's equipment. According to one principal, a teacher at his school was "abused" until he told her to stop troubleshooting. "She was being treated as a repair person," he explained. Even when participants wanted to help other teachers, they often found that people expected too much of them. One teacher commented:

> Every time there is a problem with something, they come to us and ask us to come and help correct it. We've been very willing to go to the teachers' rooms . . . We're learning a lot by doing this, but I don't feel like I am capable of doing what I need to be doing . . . A lot of times we're not finding the answers, and I don't even know where we need to look.

Lack of Time

Since few teachers have the luxury of spending a week or a month exploring, reflecting, and interacting with other teachers, participants were excited about learning new skills during practicums and summer institutes. Unfortunately, upon returning to their schools, many teachers had little time to continue learning about technology or to develop the types of lessons they had seen in ACOT classrooms. Creating cooperative learning experiences, developing interdisciplinary projects, or setting up the classroom so students can go through "stations" can take a tremendous amount of up-front time and effort.

When asked what type of support they wanted, teachers commonly requested time. Said one teacher, "Time is the major issue . . . The traditional framework that we have is not conducive to creating and learning as you go." Although a lack of time typically did not stop teachers from carrying out the technology projects they planned while at the centers, it sometimes kept them from progressing further. One teacher explained:

> As far as anything new, it's status quo. I haven't had the time to develop any new projects; I haven't had the time to explore anything . . . nobody here told me to learn, explore, and play; they told me, "You do your job."

In addition, participants sometimes became stymied at attempts to share their experiences and knowledge when colleagues felt too pressured by time constraints and viewed technology as "just something extra added to their busy day."

THE POTENTIAL OF STAFF DEVELOPMENT

When barriers such as limited access, lack of technical support, and insufficient time could be overcome or minimized, the staff development program had a meaningful influence on teachers, their schools, and their districts. In this section teachers, coordinators, and principals reflect on the types of impact the Teacher Development Center project had at the classroom, school, and district levels.

Impact at the Classroom Level

At the classroom level, changes occurred in teachers' and students' level of technology use, in teachers' instructional practices, and in their philosophical beliefs and attitudes toward teaching.

Technology Use.   The greatest impact of the staff development program was in the nature and level of technology use in participants' classrooms. For example, novice technology users reported returning to their classrooms with a greater level of comfort. As one participant commented:

> I was a nonuser of computers. Turning one on took major effort. Now I can use one well enough for classroom use, as well as help students do essays, etc., on them.

Other novice users described using their school's computer lab differently. At one school, for example, a teacher commented that she now goes with her students to the lab rather than "sending them there and having them work with another adult."

Teachers who came into the program with some technological expertise began using technology in new ways. Some, for example, reduced the use of drill-and-practice software in favor of more sophisticated tools such as databases and spreadsheets. Many reported that as a result of participating in the project, students were "getting on the computer more" than ever before. Even teachers who were already using computers extensively in their classrooms returned from the program with additional skills and ideas. One junior high school teacher, for example, returned to her classroom and implemented projects using telecommunications, a tool she had never used before. Students in her classes began communicating with children in Japan and Nova Scotia as well as with a professor of Shakespeare in New Mexico. Through the use of telecommunications, the teacher also acquired shareware that fit into her curriculum of social studies and language arts.

In addition to gaining skills related to using specific hardware and software, teachers acquired more knowledge about available technology. And with that knowledge, they often couldn't help but purchase equipment for their own homes and classrooms. Some teachers began fund-raising projects to obtain new equipment, while others spent personal funds. For example, a coordinator reported that "one teacher was just using word processing before coming to the center. Now she has bought four computers with her own money for her classroom." Another teacher felt tempted to use funds saved for her honeymoon to purchase a computer for her home.

Like ACOT teachers (see Chapter 6), teacher development center participants found that the use of technology, as well as constructivist teaching strategies, led to higher student motivation, interest, and engagement. Teachers reported that students began writing more both on computers and with paper and pencil. Peer relations also improved in some classrooms. As one teacher reported, "Technology . . . gets students turned on, and it gets them pulling together and working as a team much more effectively than anything else."

The effect on students in special education classrooms was particularly noteworthy and sometimes surprised teachers. In one classroom, the teacher found that her special education students were more willing to read when working on the computer than when in traditional reading groups. As a preschool teacher of children with special needs reported:

> Technology has literally changed the flavor of my classroom. It's such a motivator for my special needs children, and I am getting oral language from children who were previously nonverbal . . . My kids just love it! They love being in control; they develop a sense of autonomy, competence, and soon begin relating with peers, giving them a sense of belonging.

Instructional Changes.   After observing and reflecting on a variety of teaching strategies at the teacher development centers, teachers often began using new instructional techniques. For example, some teachers tried cooperative learning for the first time, while others implemented student projects. Still others began using interdisciplinary, thematic units.

The station approach, which was particularly useful for classrooms with a limited amount of technology, became popular among participants. Although planning for this approach was labor intensive, teachers found that students responded well and that the structure ensured more equal access to technology. Often, as teachers acquired more equipment, they increased the number of stations. One teacher, for example, used the station approach before participating in the program but hadn't tried a technology station. After seeing what another participant had accomplished with one computer station, she decided to integrate technology stations into a unit on Japan. Over the course of the unit, students used both CD-ROM and laser-disc players. At computer stations, they learned vocabulary skills using computer software and viewed a multimedia project sent by a Japanese high school student.

Philosophical and Attitudinal Changes. The teacher development program also influenced many teachers' attitudes toward teaching, their self-efficacy, and their beliefs about their students. Coordinators, principals, and teachers alike reported that teachers commonly returned to their schools "all fired up." One coordinator said:

> The principal was amazed that the practicum participants came back to school excited about the changes they were going to implement in their classrooms, since at least two of the participants, according to the principal, "had not been excited in years."

Along with excitement came an increase in teacher motivation and morale. One teacher—a veteran of 25 years—said of the practicum: "It totally rejuvenated me . . . Now, I can't retire!" Some teachers also reported an increase in feelings of personal empowerment when they returned to their classrooms. For example, one teacher stated:

> I . . . gained from the training . . . a feeling of excitement and of being capable. I gained a sense of accomplishment—a feeling that helped me try new and exciting ways to use technology.

Many teachers also began to view themselves as learners again and became more willing to take risks. Sometimes the risk involved trying a new lesson or using a new piece of technology. But often the risk involved changes on a deeper, more philosophical level, such as adapting student and teacher roles. One teacher, for example, said that the most important lesson she learned was

> being able to say, "I don't know, let's try it" to students when they ask if something can be done . . . I don't always need an answer for every question a child asks. We can discover the answer together.

Similar to what ACOT teachers had experienced almost a decade earlier, becoming a learner again led many participants to reflect on their teaching techniques and to question the value of what they were doing in their classrooms (see Chapters 2 and 3). "Putting the shoe on the other foot" let teachers see the value of shifting toward a constructivist teaching approach. One teacher reflected:

> I was a wonderful presenter. I was the one doing all of the work, and consequently most of the learning. Sure, my students . . . memorized the facts for the test. But I wonder now how many of them care about really learning anything . . . I find it hard, now, to believe that I expected all those kids to sit at a desk all day long and listen to me.

Teachers not only viewed themselves differently after attending the program but often returned to their classrooms with higher expectations for their students. As one coordinator described differences she observed:

> Before Mrs. Liu studied in ACOT, students used computers for drill and practice. They were not allowed to place disks in the computers and always wrote on paper first and then typed their information using the computer. They never had the opportunity to print. Today, students compose on the computer . . . and print their work.

As teachers gained new insight into students' capabilities, they often began treating them with more genuine respect. As the principal of one teacher noted, "What has changed [in her classroom] is that the kids have more input . . . and decision-making power."

Impact at the School Level

Many participating teachers not only changed their classroom instruction but also shared what they learned with colleagues at their schools. Others went a step further and took more formal leadership roles, ultimately influencing their schools' or districts' climate and vision for the future.

Teachers as Staff Developers and Technology Trainers. Upon returning to their schools, many teachers began sharing their new skills and ideas with colleagues. They conducted miniworkshops and in-service sessions, made presentations to faculty members and parents' groups, and held open houses where they demonstrated their new skills with technology. These teachers seemed anxious to share their expertise with others, even when it meant working increasingly long hours before and after school. As one teacher stated, "I see my job as continuing to help other teachers and sharing with them what I've done."

Participants shared their newfound expertise not only with other teachers but with students as well. At one school, a teacher held one-hour sessions every week after school for 15 weeks to train teachers and two students from every class on computer basics, curriculum integration, and software programs. At another school, two teachers taught students in the gifted program how to use technology, including various software programs and camcorders. The students then went into other classrooms to teach their peers. Based on the enthusiastic response to this project, the teachers convinced the principal to buy a site license for a software program that they planned to integrate into the science curriculum.

Some teachers designed projects that involved the entire school in learning technology. One teacher, for example, gathered all the computers not being used and made a lab in the library. The entire school staff began coming through the lab to work on keyboarding with their classes. Similarly, another teacher organized a school project that taught students from different grade levels how to use a hypermedia application. Older students learned from kindergarten and first-grade students as they jointly created a multimedia presentation for a tribute to the principal.

Participating teachers also involved parents and other community members. After holding a school in-service session that was poorly attended by staff members, the school media specialist focused on parents instead and trained them to help in the library and in classrooms. At another school, participants organized a multimedia fair that was open to the community. Since this event was so well attended, teachers planned an even bigger fair for the next year.

Teachers also devised informal strategies for enticing reluctant teachers into the world of technology. Several teachers, for example, put up bulletin boards in the halls for other students and teachers to see how technology was used in their classrooms. They found that the bulletin boards "really seemed to get lots of teachers interested to see what we were doing." At one school, another teacher took a minimalist approach to working with his colleagues. Rather than trying to impress them with the most sophisticated uses of technology that he had learned, he decided to "show exactly the lowest level of what you can do for yourself on the computer." After informally showing four or five teachers the minimum information needed to set up the computer to produce a newsletter, he hooked teachers into learning more. He said, "They realized a lot of it is very easy . . . I had more teachers come back to me and say, 'Gosh, this was the first time we've ever had anybody sit down and slowly explain it to us.'"

Other teachers didn't need to be enticed to learn about technology use. Once the opportunity was there, word got around. For example, after inviting a few colleagues to observe a lesson using technology, one teacher found that others started coming in to watch and to borrow equipment. Principals repeatedly commented that once participating teachers started the process of change at their schools, "other teachers who had never expressed interest in technology before [began] to jump on the bandwagon."

Teachers as Leaders. Principals reported that participating teachers, upon returning to their schools, often took on leadership roles that ultimately affected the school's climate and mission. After visiting the teacher development centers, teachers wanted more training and more technology for their classrooms and used a variety of strategies to get what they wanted.

Some teachers joined or formed school technology committees and began to push their colleagues to create a shared vision for technology use throughout the school. In some cases, these committees found local organizations to help fund technology acquisition or organize fund-raising efforts. A number of participants successfully convinced parent groups or principals to allocate their funds for technology rather than other purposes. One principal commented, "There used to be a lot of resistance in the PTA toward computers. Now the attitude has changed." At another school, the principal used funds from a program for gifted students to hire substitutes for the participating teachers, who wanted time away from regular classroom duties to teach gifted students how to use technology.

Other teachers convinced principals to change their spending priorities. One principal jokingly said of his teachers, "Now they want more technology . . . It's kind of like giving an alcoholic a drink. Sending teachers to the center cost me a lot of money!" Principals also looked to participating teachers for help with decisions about technology purchasing and acquisition. One teacher, for example, reported:

> My principal called me in . . . and said that we have money . . . he wants to spend it on technology. He wanted me to go ahead and start making decisions as to how that should best be done. . . We have gone through catalogues, we have asked other ACOT-trained

teachers for input. . . This was an awesome task, but I do feel like the training I had this summer did help me in making those decisions.

Teachers began writing grant proposals to acquire more technology and successfully obtained small grants from local foundations as well as larger grants from the district and state. For example, one district awarded incentive grants to 15 schools; 10 of these schools had sent teachers to the staff development program. Fourteen schools also obtained state grants after participating teachers assisted in writing the proposals. Principals at some of these schools acknowledged that the proposals probably would not have been written if the teacher development center participants "hadn't insisted on it." Teachers agreed. One stated:

> My exposure to the teacher development program, along with [that of] several coworkers, led to major changes in our school's technological future. We have gotten over $200,000 worth of technology for our school in the past year through grants and PTA support.

Another exclaimed:

> We applied for . . . and have received a $50,000 grant to equip the classroom . . . Prior to attending the center, I would never have dared to dream so big or known how to try to accomplish my dream!

Graduates of the Teacher Development Center project also took on leadership roles beyond their schools. For instance, a local university invited two teachers to conduct a technology-related summer school class for preservice teachers. At another site, teachers helped teach district in-service workshops on technology-related topics. Participating teachers also made presentations to principals' groups, a situation that reversed traditional roles. These types of experiences provided informal recognition of teachers' expertise and encouraged further professional development.

SUPPORTS FOR CHANGE

The teachers who made the most changes were those who had the greatest level of support. Supports included assistance from project coordinators, other teachers who participated in the teacher development program, and school and district administrators.

Coordinator Support

New skills need to be reinforced. Teachers, like students, cannot be expected to engage in new skills or behaviors unless they have feedback and support soon after they are introduced to the new activity. We found that teachers' excitement and enthusiasm about integrating technology often faded if they did not receive support within a few weeks of attending the staff development program. For this reason, project coordinators offered participants ongoing support for one year. Because of time constraints, coordinators typically visited teachers at their schools a few times over the course of the year, but they offered less formal support over the telephone, through telecommunications, and at user group meetings. The coordinators' support took a variety of forms—from helping to set up hardware to discussing school technology goals with the principal to providing advice on grant writing.

Teachers appreciated the encouragement, feedback, and new ideas coordinators gave them:

> The coordinator just gets you so excited because she's so excited that you've done your project . . . That just gets you that much more turned on. It's not just that you're doing it to please her, but it just gets you to want to do more.

In addition to helping individual participants, coordinators also served as advisors to the schools, making presentations to technology committees, parent groups, and sometimes entire faculties. Commonly, coordinators held in-service training for the full staff or helped the school develop a technology plan. As one coordinator said, each school that sent participants is "part of the family," so she did not hesitate to help anyone at that school, whether or not they attended the Teacher Development Center project.

Besides getting assistance from the coordinator, participating teachers turned to each other for help with troubleshooting equipment, for lesson ideas, and for emotional support, similar to their ACOT predecessors (see Chapter 7). This type of camaraderie—which often made the difference between a computer sitting idly and successful technology use—was not limited to teams of teachers from within a particular school, but included teacher development center graduates from schools throughout the country. Informal teacher networks emerged at each site. Some teachers communicated by phone, while others used telecommunications. Still others met on a regular basis to share success stories, demonstrate new skills, and receive additional training. For some teachers, participation in the staff development program served to whet their appetite for new learning, and they were not shy about asking for additional support, as this entry from a coordinator's journal illustrates:

> I'm also going to start weekly meetings with the [center] teachers at our school . . . They want extra training, and they want to look at this or want to try that, or they want to exchange ideas . . . these people being in the school have some expectations of more contact, more support.

Administrative Support

Lack of access, inadequate technical support, and insufficient time for teacher learning and planning are barriers that need to be addressed at school and district levels. Consistent with research investigating teacher change (Office of Technology Assessment, 1995), we found that the most crucial determining factor in whether participating teachers integrated technology into their classrooms and moved toward a constructivist teaching approach was the level of support they received from school and district administrators. While principal support was theoretically a prerequisite for attending the teacher development center, principals varied dramatically in their attitudes toward technology and in what actions they took to help teachers. The following excerpts, taken from coordinator reports, illustrate the range of administrative support participants experienced. One teacher told the coordinator:

> The principal knows nothing about the use of technology and is scared to learn . . . He was the principal that told me when I notified him his school would be one of the weeklong participating schools this year that he really did not want it. He also stated he applied last year and was relieved when he did not receive it.

In contrast, another teacher reported:

> The principal has arranged for his entire faculty to receive training with the university on a telecommunications project by running telephone lines and computers into the gym on a designated Saturday . . . He bought a portable computer and

presently has 14 megabytes of RAM on it. He almost gets as excited about the use of technology as I do.

While one principal was willing to sleep on the school roof to raise money for computers, others did not live up to the commitment given to teachers before they visited the centers. At one school, for example, the principal reneged on providing computers for participants, telling them to use the school lab. A teacher from another school commented, "I've been told that I'll have to spend my own money on software. No one from the administration looked at my project, although they were invited." Actions such as these send important messages to teachers and can make or break efforts to change.

Providing Time for Learning.   Principals and district administrators seeking school change also benefit from arranging time for teachers to continue their professional development. Learning how to use technology and to teach with a constructivist approach cannot be mastered in a one-shot workshop, regardless of its length. Providing release time for teachers, even if only a few hours a month, is an effective way of promoting continued growth.

Showing Interest.   Administrators don't have to be "technology gurus" themselves to provide support for teachers, but they should show interest in what teachers are learning. Coordinators found when principals attended part or all of the practicums, teachers felt a greater level of support. As one coordinator commented, "When the principal is there . . . there is bonding. Otherwise, there are questions in teachers' minds about what support they will get when they return to their schools."

Arranging Technical Support.   Although teachers can troubleshoot and help their peers, those who are teaching full-time should not be expected to be technicians. Few schools can provide teachers with full-time, on-site technical support; but as schools get more technology, administrators should consider investing in technology support rather than putting all of their funds into hardware and software.

Easing Access Problems.   Administrators can ease access problems by finding creative ways to fund technology purchases and by making technology acquisition a priority. Many participants' principals reevaluated school budgets and found ways to buy equipment. One principal, who described his school as "poor as Job's turkey," put phone lines in classrooms so teachers could use telecommunications. He stated, "I am gung-ho about technology. I've seen the world change." Another principal used profits from a fund-raising carnival to buy a site license for a grading program; he saw this as a way of enticing all teachers at his school to use technology. In schools with this type of leadership, access improved and the staff development project had a stronger impact.

In contrast, access remained problematic in schools and districts where issues of equity were paramount. At some schools, principals refused to give teacher development center participants more equipment until everyone at the school had the same level of technology, even if this policy meant that computers would be sitting unused in classrooms of teachers who did not want, or know how, to use them. At one school, for example, the principal believed that everyone should have a computer, so hardware was distributed equally as it became available regardless of teachers' level of interest in or commitment to using technology. Similarly, district administrators prohibited schools that had received state or district grants from sending participants to the teacher development center unless the openings could not be filled by other schools. And, even if teachers from schools receiving these state or district grants did attend summer institutes, they would not be given a computer from their district or Apple Computer.

Access can often be increased when teachers are willing to share technology. Sharing can be facilitated by putting computers on movable carts as well as by using portable technology, such as laptop computers. However, sharing equipment can be a scheduling headache for teachers, and if equipment must be moved on heavy carts in short periods of time (such as between periods at the high school level), teachers are less likely to use it.

Creating a Shared School Vision. Concerns about equity can often be alleviated when administrators and staff create a shared school vision. When staff members are working toward common, agreed-upon goals, perceived inequities are less likely to hinder school change. Several participants felt that the lack of a shared school vision seriously hampered their progress. One stated:

We have our cliques, divisions . . . We're all kind of doing our own thing and we're not working together. And it's high time we come together and have a meeting of the minds—a decision of where are we going to go from here.

Unfortunately, reaching consensus is often difficult. In one school, for example, two summer institute participants disagreed about whether computer equipment should be kept in a lab or distributed to classrooms. The ensuing conflict led one of the teachers to transfer to another school. Elsewhere, coprincipals had different ideas on which direction their school should go with regard to technology use. In situations such as these, maintaining the status quo was usually the result.

Sometimes, principals are reluctant to share decision-making power with teachers. In one school, for example, teachers wanted computers put into the classrooms, while the principal wanted to create a lab. Ultimately, a lab was assembled. Teachers expressed disappointment but not surprise: "The principal makes the final decision on everything." When teachers feel that their input is not valued, they are likely to resist changes that administrators want to implement. By genuinely collaborating with their staff to create a shared school vision, school administrators can ease tensions with teachers and foster shared decision making.

11

Technology: One Tool
Among Many

❝ *Technology has its foot in the door of classrooms all across America, and the schools will never be the same.* ❞ — Mehlinger, 1996, p. 406

❝ *[T]he lure of computer technology has a magic air about it. Faced with silvery discs with rainbow hues and an abstract highway that makes the yellow brick road seem mundane, the uninitiated may find it hard to question the legitimacy of the movement, much less say no or whoa to it . . . The technology-as-magic elixir approach is dangerous and unjustified by the evidence.* ❞
— Pepi & Scheurman, 1996, pp. 230–231

What potential does technology have for transforming teaching and learning? The authors just quoted have contrasting outlooks about the promise of technology. The first is optimistic that technology will positively change schools, but the second is skeptical and exhortative about technology's role.

Over the past 10 years, ACOT has investigated how routine use of technology by teachers and students affects teaching and learning. This research suggests that the impact of technology on education lies somewhere between these two positions. Technology has potential to change education in beneficial ways, but only under certain circumstances. In some classrooms computers sit idle, becoming expensive "dust collectors." In others, computers are used as glorified electronic workbooks, primarily for drill and practice. In ACOT classrooms, however, the introduction of technology fundamentally altered teaching and learning. Students routinely used technological tools to collect, organize, and analyze data; to enhance presentations; to conduct simulations; and to solve complex problems.

What factors contribute to these different levels of use? Numerous barriers can inhibit the successful integration of technology. Some problems relate to the physical structure of the school, such as inadequate electrical wiring or lack of a telephone line, and can be easily remedied if funds are available. Many other obstacles are not so easy to remove, however, because they are deeply embedded in the institutional structure of the school itself: curricular mandates that focus on learning discrete facts rather than problem solving, assessment based on test performance rather than the learning process, rules and regulations that reward teacher compliance rather than risk taking. Even more difficult to overcome are barriers that are in the minds of teachers—deeply held beliefs about teacher and student roles, about the nature of learning and instruction, and even about technology itself.

This chapter examines key conditions that are necessary for technology to improve education. First, the successful use of technology—or the adoption of any educational innovation—requires teachers to confront their beliefs about learning and the efficacy of different instructional activities. Second, technology should be viewed as one tool among many and will have little influence unless it is successfully integrated into a meaningful curricular and instructional framework. Third, teachers need to work in contexts that support risk taking and experimentation, and that provide opportunities for collegial sharing and ongoing professional growth. Fourth, although technology can serve as a catalyst for change, the process of technology integration should be viewed as a long-term, challenging enterprise.

CHANGING TEACHERS' BELIEFS

Teachers are, by the nature of their work, pragmatists. They must survive the day; they must be ready for the next. Confronted by large numbers of computers or not, they arrive at their classrooms the first day of their careers with beliefs about schooling well in mind, beliefs built from stories heard from parents and older siblings, beliefs built from years of participating in one particular kind of schooling, beliefs that will help them weather the storm of demands they face.

These beliefs about schooling, built over years in the minds of those who come to teach and sanctioned by those who already teach, lead to a seeming contradiction. While those who talk *about* schooling describe its penchant for change, teachers who *do* schooling proceed about their business in a manner that is remarkably resistant to change. Our research suggests that the introduction of technology to classrooms does not radically change teaching; instead, technology can serve as a symbol of change, granting teachers a license for experimentation.

For ACOT teachers, learning to integrate technology into instruction and adopting constructivist teaching strategies involved experimenting with new ideas and ways of operating until old habits gave way to new. As they successfully attempted new methods of instruction, they saw for themselves the value of strategies such as peer tutoring and collaboration and began to reevaluate their beliefs about learning and teaching. In this process, ACOT teachers created a new culture in their classrooms. It was a slow, difficult, and, we believe, critically important pursuit that led them through five stages of instructional evolution.

In the entry stage of the ACOT project, participating teachers had little or no experience with computer technology and demonstrated little inclination to significantly change their instruction. The first weeks of the project involved transforming the physical environment to accommodate the influx of technology. Once instruction began, veteran teachers faced typical beginning-teacher problems such as discipline, resource management, and personal frustration. Teachers began using their technological resources, but simply to replicate traditional instructional activities. As teachers moved into the adoption stage, their concerns shifted from connecting the computers to using them. Teachers adopted the new electronic technology to support their established text-based, drill-and-practice instruction. Students continued to receive steady diets of whole-group lectures, recitation, and individualized seat work. Although the physical environments had changed, the instructional strategies remained the same, just using different tools.

The adaptation phase brought changes in the efficiency of the instructional process. Student productivity increased in a variety of areas, and teachers noted improved student engagement in classroom tasks. As teachers eventually reached the appropriation and invention stages, they came to understand technology and use it effortlessly as a tool. Their roles began to shift noticeably, and new instructional patterns emerged. Team teaching, interdisciplinary project-based instruction, and individually paced instruction became more common. To accommodate more ambitious class projects, teachers even altered the master schedule. Perhaps most important, teachers reflected on their teaching, questioned old patterns, and speculated about the causes behind the changes they were seeing in their students.

As teachers moved through these stages, they naturally vacillated between instructional approaches that had worked for years and new strategies that seemed more appropriate in their technology-rich classrooms. Much of the vacillation related to dilemmas that emerged—dilemmas that stemmed more from long-held beliefs than from problems inherent to using technology. For instance, when teachers shifted from the belief that learning activities needed to be divided into discrete subject areas, they incorporated more project-based instruction and became less concerned that the technology was taking time away from other subjects. When teachers moved away from the view of teacher as expert and their classrooms became more student directed, concerns about student experimentation and disruption of teacher plans diminished.

These shifts in beliefs occurred as teachers began to see benefits for both themselves and their students. Over time, teachers personally appropriated technology for creative expression and personal work, and they used it to their advantage in managing the classroom and preparing for instruction. Teachers began to work together in teams, leading to new instructional ideas and increasing their interactions with and support from their colleagues. Teachers felt revitalized when they viewed themselves as learners again, and their use of technology increased their sense of professionalism and achievement. Moreover, they witnessed benefits for their students that rewarded teachers' efforts. For example, students demonstrated a steady interest in technology and used it more frequently and imaginatively as their technical competence increased. Their productivity increased, and they wrote more fluently. As students selected and used appropriate technological tools, problem-solving and thinking skills developed. Cooperative and task-related interaction among students was spontaneous, and more extensive than in regular classrooms.

In addition, teachers had higher expectations of what students could accomplish. Many lower-achieving students positively responded to alternative means of expressing their knowledge, raising their self-esteem as well as their status with peers and teachers. By incorporating different instructional styles, teachers managed to reach students who had not excelled using traditional approaches. One teacher, for example, reflected on her early efforts to use project-based instruction and on the different ways students responded to this teaching method:

> Some kids who are model students when the task is straightforward, such as a fill-in-the-blanks kind of thing, are having a tremendously difficult time dealing with such an open-ended task as this. It's like they are lost, not knowing where to begin or how to proceed. At the same time, [others,] who with a worksheet are perpetually off task, have plunged on ahead, eagerly producing some original and outstanding projects. It indicates how our instructional style favors some individuals over others and how a traditional instructional approach hampers some students we consider very able.

We witnessed similar transformations in the classrooms of participants of the Teacher Development Center project, even though most of these teachers had far less access to technology than did ACOT teachers. Novice users began to use technology more frequently in their classrooms. More experienced users reduced their reliance on drill-and-practice programs and began using more sophisticated tool software. Some teachers began questioning their traditional instructional approaches and started to implement constructivist teaching strategies. Still others began to see themselves as learners and felt a sense of excitement and rejuvenation. In many cases, teachers reported that the changes they had instituted had a positive impact on their students, such as increased engagement and motivation and improvements in students' abilities to work together. These changes were more likely in classrooms where teachers used technology as a tool and integrated it into the larger curricular and instructional framework.

USING TECHNOLOGY WITHIN THE CURRICULAR FRAMEWORK

In line with ACOT's vision, we view technology as a powerful tool for teaching and learning. However, despite its potential, technology can never replace teachers, as some people predicted when computers were first introduced to classrooms. While the role of computers should go well beyond being teaching machines, technology is only one tool among many. As such, it should be used only when it is the most appropriate means of reaching a learning goal.

As one tool among many, technology cannot be expected to change bad teaching into good. In fact, technology can make good teaching better or bad teaching worse. The basic approach to teaching and learning that is being implemented in the classroom is far more important than whether or not technology is used. Teachers' prior practices have more influence on how technology will be used than the technology itself (Fosnot, 1992; Miller & Olson, 1995). The most critical issue is how technology fits into the larger curricular and instructional framework.

Technology is most powerful when used with constructivist teaching approaches that emphasize problem solving, concept development, and critical thinking rather than simple acquisition of factual knowledge. In this framework, learning is viewed as something a learner does, not something that is done *to* a learner (Fosnot, 1989). Despite the importance of constructivist strategies, we believe the most effective teachers are those who can implement a variety of approaches for the benefit of their students and reach a balance between instruction and construction activities.

Technology and Teacher-Directed Instruction

In numerous elementary and high school classrooms, however, the lecture–recitation–seat work model predominates. Also, at the university level, direct instruction is relied upon almost exclusively. These approaches remain the dominant modes of teaching for a several reasons. First, some feel that these are the best teaching methods.

Students are easier to control when they are sitting in their seats, listening to a teacher lecture, answering questions, or completing worksheets. Lecturing is appealing to teachers, particularly at the secondary and college levels, because it makes direct use of their subject matter expertise and allows them to cover material more quickly than with other instructional approaches. Many students also find it easier to be passive recipients of information than to be actively involved and responsible for their own learning. As one teacher beginning to use technology noted, "If I am not standing up in front, talking, then the kids don't think I'm teaching."

Second, people tend to teach as they were taught. This tendency showed up even among the students in the ACOT classrooms. For example, when teaching each other how to use the technology, students naturally used hands-on instruction. However, when they began to teach one another content information, students resorted to a lecture-presentation mode.

Finally, the process of planning and implementing didactic instructional approaches is often less time consuming than using other teaching methods. Teachers who use project-based, interdisciplinary, thematic, cooperative, and other types of instructional approaches (alone or in combination) comment consistently on how much more time it takes to prepare and carry out learning activities.

Our position is that the lecture–recitation–seat work model and direct instruction are appropriate for certain activities, such as for presenting factual information, introducing skills and concepts, or when breadth is valued over depth. However, when computers are used to replicate these traditional patterns of instruction, the potential power of technology is wasted. "Real school" continues, but with a slight technological twist—drill and practice on a computer.

In addition, the potential of technology goes unrealized if a teacher's goal is to "teach technology." Frequently, advocates of technology use in classrooms cite the importance of students developing job skills, and teachers sometimes respond by using technology to teach keyboarding and word processing rather than using it as a tool to teach the curriculum. Yet at the rate that technology changes, a broader goal is more relevant to job preparation—that is, to help students become comfortable with using technology and to understand ways in which technology may be most helpful. Locating and accessing information, organizing and displaying data, creating persuasive arguments, and dynamically demonstrating ideas and conclusions to critical audiences of peers will be more useful job skills than knowing the actual mechanics of specific hardware and software that will quickly be obsolete. When technology is integrated into the larger instructional framework, students will learn how to use the equipment and software in addition to even more valuable skills.

Technology and Student-Centered Instruction

The benefits of technology integration are best realized when learning is not just the process of transferring facts from one person to another, but when the teacher's goal is to empower students as thinkers and problem solvers. Technology provides an excellent platform—a conceptual environment—where children can collect information in multiple formats and then organize, visualize, link, and discover relationships among facts and events. Students can use the same technologies to communicate their ideas to others, to argue and critique their perspectives, to persuade and teach others, and to add greater levels of understanding to their growing knowledge.

Software designed specifically for educational purposes often focuses on basic skill development. By contrast, tool software such as word processing, databases, spreadsheets, hypermedia applications, and multimedia can lead to opportunities for student problem solving and critical thinking. In the following example, an ACOT teacher reflected on the usefulness of a hypermedia application for enhancing student understanding:

> One student has begun to develop a hypermedia stack to illustrate the types of radioactive decay. As she was drawing the stack, she noticed some things that she would not have otherwise noticed . . . The way the decay process occurred and how effective the arrangement of the atoms and the lack of symmetry of the particles of an atom became clear as she analyzed the parts of the illustration in order to convert it into an animated form on the computer. It was interesting the things that stood out and became more evident and clear to her that she would have otherwise missed if she had not been producing a hypermedia stack.

Technology used in meaningful ways such as this can transform student learning, as we witnessed in the ACOT classrooms. At the high school, for example, students composed gothic short stories on the computer, adding a sense of mystery with multimedia effects. Students collaboratively solved algebra problems, exchanged homework, and critiqued each other's solutions. Sometimes they built hypermedia stacks that demonstrated problem-solving techniques for use as tutorials for other students. At examination time, students often downloaded tests from the network and proceeded to solve problems that were evaluated as they worked. Groups of students created multimedia presentations about diverse topics—everything from Chinese history to First Amendment rights to the works of French and Spanish artists (written in French and Spanish). At times, students worked on whole-class interdisciplinary projects.

At elementary and middle-grade levels, teachers balanced traditional recitation and seat work with interdisciplinary, project-based instruction that integrated the same advanced technology used in the high school classes. For instance, middle-grade students worked with a professional scientific visualization tool developed by the National Institutes of Health. They also solved problems using planetary images downloaded from satellites and visual data sets from government agencies that make current data accessible to schools. When a hurricane ravaged the East Coast, students used digital satellite images and National Weather Service maps to track the storm and to determine the multiple forces that interact to drive hurricanes across the face of the planet. Elementary children practiced basic skills, including keyboarding, at individualized rates. Using a variety of word-processing software, students composed reports on computers and then produced them using desktop publishing programs. Other times, they produced their reports using video cameras.

This move away from teacher-directed instruction to student-centered learning does not lessen teachers' responsibilities, as this teacher noted:

> Constructivism cannot replace "teaching" . . . but others do interpret it as a replacement for teaching. Children need more. We cannot abandon our responsibility to teach, which some think we do in the name of constructivism.

In fact, designing and implementing units such as those described above typically require more time and effort than traditional lessons. Although technology can facilitate constructivist teaching, using this approach is difficult unless teachers are supported in their efforts. The following section describes some of the supports that teachers need to integrate technology successfully into the larger curricular and instructional framework.

THE IMPORTANCE OF A SUPPORTIVE CONTEXT

The effective use of technology involves much more than adding computers to classrooms. Typically, however, schools and districts allocate most of their funds for purchasing hardware and software, and much less—if anything—is designated for teacher professional development and ongoing support. The instructional evolution we witnessed in ACOT classrooms was a result of not only ACOT teachers' hard work and dedication, but also the contextual supports that they received from the project and from their schools and districts. Even with a high level of support, classroom change was slow and challenging. Without this support, purchasing hardware and software may be a poor investment.

ACOT staff built a variety of supports for teachers into the project—such as constant access to technology; technical and instructional support; technical training; and release time for joint planning, discussions, and team teaching. Teachers also benefited from using a telecommunications network that allowed interaction across sites and with ACOT project staff. A full-time coordinator worked at each site, providing a high level of technical and instructional assistance.

At some sites, schools and districts also provided support to the ACOT teachers. Administrators often publicly recognized and encouraged their efforts and tried to decrease their workloads by relieving them of school- and district-level responsibilities. At the high school site, administrators allowed teachers to use block scheduling, facilitating project-based, interdisciplinary instruction. They also supported teachers' attempts to try new approaches with technology and encouraged risk taking and experimentation.

ACOT staff learned that the types of supports teachers needed varied, depending on where they were in their instructional evolution (see Table 3.1). For example, teachers in the entry stage needed a greater amount of technical support and help with troubleshooting. By contrast, in the adaptation stage, teachers wanted to learn about alternative teaching strategies. ACOT staff also discovered that teachers needed ongoing support. Even teachers who had been with the project for years and had reached the invention stage sought continued opportunities for professional development.

Perhaps the most important type of support that teachers received was not from ACOT staff but from each other. In the process of change, ACOT teachers turned to their colleagues for emotional, technical, and instructional support. They collaborated together, shared ideas for specific lessons, and taught each other new skills. As a result of this camaraderie, ACOT teachers who joined the project in later years moved more quickly through the evolutionary stages. Veteran ACOT teachers modeled new instructional approaches, and the new teachers could see for themselves how ACOT students benefited.

Applying the Principles of Support

The knowledge that ACOT staff gained about teacher change and the types of ongoing supports teachers need to progress through the evolutionary stages was directly applied to the design of the ACOT teacher development centers. ACOT required participants to attend in teams of two to four so that they could support each other. While at the center, participants spent much of their time working and observing in ACOT classrooms, where ACOT teachers modeled different instructional approaches and students demonstrated their skills. Participants reflected upon and articulated their beliefs about instruction, assessment, and technology during group discussions and journal writing. Rather than relying on a didactic approach, coordinators encouraged participants to learn how to use technology by working side by side with each other, by exploring on their own, or by working with ACOT students. The teacher development centers modeled the type of learning environment that is advocated by the project.

When Teacher Development Center project participants returned to their schools, their struggles to implement change in their classrooms reaffirmed our views about the importance of contextual supports. Teachers who had little or no access to appropriate hardware and software were unlikely to integrate technology into their instruction. When technology was relegated only to labs, teachers were more likely to view it as an add-on to an already full curriculum, and less likely to use it. Teachers who had no time to explore, learn new skills, or plan new lessons tended to maintain the status quo. And when teachers found that their technology was not working properly in the middle of a lesson, and had no help in fixing the problem, they were reluctant to take further risks.

While teacher development center coordinators helped many teachers overcome barriers, their support alone was generally not sufficient to sustain teacher change. We found that administrative support was crucial in determining whether or not teachers would implement what they had learned while at the teacher development centers. For example, by making technology use a priority, administrators reduced such problems as insufficient time for continued learning, limited access, and lack of technical support. While schools may not have budgeted for these types of support, committed administrators found ways to reprioritize the school's budget or managed to obtain financial resources from grants, businesses, and the local community.

Although some contextual supports were difficult and expensive to implement, administrators provided others relatively easily and with no cost. For example, teachers were unlikely to change when they felt others were uninterested in their ideas and input, or were jealous of them. However, by showing interest in changes teachers were instituting in their classrooms, school administrators offered their teachers much needed emotional and moral support. By encouraging participants to take positions of leadership, they increased the likelihood that participants would share what they had learned with their colleagues. Finally, by working with their staff to create a shared vision for the future, they eased tensions among teachers and fostered teacher collaboration rather than competition.

Support Within the Larger Educational Context

However, administrative support at the school level is not enough when the larger context of district, state, and national policies inhibits rather than encourages change. For example, one of the most serious systemic barriers to the transformation we witnessed in ACOT classrooms was student and teacher assessment. When students demonstrated new learning outcomes, such as creative problem-solving strategies or heightened abilities to collaborate in performing tasks, their teachers struggled with how to translate those demonstrations into quantitative measures that could be entered into grade books. Rewarding students for their successes with the new competencies proved difficult. These outcomes cannot be easily measured on standardized tests. Most tests measure basic recall or simple computational or factual knowledge. Assessing the understanding of concepts and problem-solving skills is much more difficult. But the emphasis on accountability encourages teachers to teach toward the goal of improving test scores. Teachers using alternative approaches need other ways to measure student progress.

Teacher evaluation proved similarly problematic. In defense of their own careers, ACOT teachers sometimes interrupted the natural flow of project-based activities to "demonstrate" whole-class direct instruction for the benefit of district evaluators, whose instruments were too inflexible to accommodate more active classroom environments. In one instance, an evaluator told the teacher to have him return on a day when he could observe her "actually teaching." When being evaluated, "teachers are reinforced for efficient 'covering' of the curriculum, smoothly managed classrooms, and skilled imitation of clichéd ways of teaching. Teachers' energies are spent on imitating rather than on thinking" (Fosnot, 1989, p. 7). Technology will have a limited impact on education when teacher evaluation is limited to assessing how well teachers deliver direct instruction.

The process of evaluating teaching or assessing student learning is linked to people's beliefs about what constitutes effective teaching. Before we can expect to see significant change in these and other areas of educational policy and practice, we will need to see corresponding changes in the educational community's beliefs about teachers' roles and effective teaching. However, as we witnessed with ACOT teachers, changing beliefs require a high level of support and a great deal of time.

TAKING A LONG-TERM PERSPECTIVE

The experience of the ACOT project demonstrates the value of taking a long-term perspective on change. Unfortunately, most studies of the effects of technology focus on a specific intervention and on short-term results; though interesting, these types of short-term studies are of marginal value to policymakers (Mehlinger, 1996). ACOT research provides a much needed longitudinal perspective on technology use in classrooms. Had we examined teachers' experiences for only a year or two, our conclusions would have been significantly different. Essentially, we would have seen frustration mixed with sincere attempts to integrate technology but little substantial change in classroom practice.

By studying teachers' experiences in technology-rich classrooms over numerous years, we recognize several reasons for taking a long-term position on change. First, even when classroom environments are drastically altered and teachers are willingly immersed in innovation, change is slow and sometimes includes temporary regression. Yet frequently those funding or evaluating innovative programs expect to see measurable progress in a short time, often adding pressure rather than providing support.

Second, teacher commitment to an innovation will not occur until they see positive benefits for themselves and their students. As demonstrated in the ACOT classrooms, the process of integrating technology into classroom instruction initially increases teachers' workloads and creates additional management problems. Moreover, the process involves gradual shifts in both beliefs and practices. Teachers need time to explore, experiment, reflect, evaluate, and revise. Over time, the benefits become obvious and compelling, and over time, lasting changes occur. By looking over the long term, obstacles are minimized and benefits become significant.

Third, the contextual supports necessary to promote teacher change are rarely in place when technology is added to schools. Although teachers are central to change, it is equally important that parents, administrators, and policymakers understand and support these shifts in beliefs and practices. They set boundaries for teachers, schools, and districts, just as teachers set limits for students and their classrooms.

Fourth, shifts in the larger sphere of teacher professional development are occurring even more slowly than in the classrooms of individual teachers. Consequently, teachers have few models of successful technology integration to draw upon as they prepare to become teachers and launch their teaching careers. Most teacher education programs offer educational computing courses that emphasize fundamental computer operation, word-processing, and basic educational uses; but few programs are actively exploring integrating technology into methods courses and student-teaching activities, and even fewer have planned for and integrated technology across the curriculum (Willis & Mehlinger, 1996). In addition, teacher education faculty are not exemplars of technology use: "They did not see its use modeled by the faculty who taught them, and they have not received much in-service training or support at the institutions where they teach" (p. 1020). Equally important are the access to and use of technology at the sites where preservice teachers complete their field experience. The initial training is most effective when student teachers subsequently have the opportunity to work with veteran teachers who regularly use technology in their classrooms. Similarly, as illustrated by the teachers who participated in the ACOT Teacher Development Center project, in-service staff development is more relevant when teachers see technology integration modeled by other teachers in classroom settings.

Not only can teachers serve as models for each other, their experiences can give teachers who are learning to use technology a road map for the process. By knowing what to expect, teachers can more easily maneuver around the obstacles and more quickly reach their destination.

TEACHERS AS THE GATEWAY TO CHANGE

Teachers are frequently targeted for criticism when there are problems in schools, but they are rarely asked for solutions. Yet their views, beliefs, and actions are of paramount significance. Ultimately, teachers decide what happens within their own classrooms. Consequently, teachers are the gateway to change (Cuban, 1986). Their direct involvement in reform efforts can provide the impetus and direction for change. For when the questions are classroom based and teacher driven, the solutions also are classroom based and teacher driven.

As we have seen throughout this book, the addition of technology can exacerbate or enhance the already complex challenge of teaching. Teachers who are willing to invest the time and effort that is needed to innovate deserve support. For this reason, we offer the following guiding principles (Table 11.1) to teachers, schools, and districts interested in supporting technology integration, and encourage them to adapt these principles to local needs and conditions.

Table 11.1   Core principles for supporting technology integration

Technology

Technology is viewed as a catalyst and tool for reengaging teachers and children in the excitement of learning and for making that learning more relevant to the 21st century. But technology is not a magic bullet—it is only one necessary ingredient in reform efforts.

Technology is most powerfully used as a new tool to support student inquiry, composition, collaboration, and communication.

Rather than being taught separately, technology should be integrated into the larger instructional and curricular framework.

Students need adequate access to technology, including classroom-based machines and additional portable resources that can be shared among classes.

Technology is best learned within the context of meaningful tasks.

Learning

Learning is an active and social process that occurs best in environments that are student centered, where teachers take facilitative roles to guide students in meaningful inquiries, where discovering relationships among facts is valued more than memorizing the facts themselves, and where knowledge building activities

are balanced with the sensible use of guided practice and direct instruction.

New competencies such as abilities to collaborate, to recognize and analyze problems as systems, to acquire and use large amounts of information, and to apply technology to the solution of real-world problems are valued outcomes.

(table continues overleaf)

Table 11.1 Core principles for supporting technology integration *(continued)*

Professional Development

Teachers are most willing to adopt and adapt new ideas when they are modeled in active classrooms where students are successfully engaged.

Professional growth is accelerated in contexts where teachers work as teams and engage in reflective, collegial patterns of work focused on the development of new learning tasks, situations, interactions, tools, and assessments for their own classrooms.

Application of new skills in teachers' own classrooms is most likely when follow-up—coaching and opportunities for reflection—begins soon after the professional development experience.

Continued growth occurs where teachers develop support teams with whom they discuss and critique practice on a regular basis.

Throughout this book we have drawn upon the voices of teachers themselves to illustrate the types of concerns teachers face and the benefits they accrue when integrating technology into their daily classroom instruction. Recognizing the importance of teachers' points of view, we conclude the book as we began—with a teacher's voice. Her words embody several fundamental points about the potential for teaching with technology. In her reflection, the teacher points out the reliance on lecture and how it diminishes active participation by students. She talks about teachers' limited role in decisions about curriculum in contrast to teachers' ability to alter classroom instruction. And she describes how technology can be used either to maintain the status quo or to promote more active, student-centered instruction.

> Being on hall duty this year, I have a chance to hear how, in class after class, the teacher's voice drones on and on and on. There is very little chance for the student to become an active participant. In today's schools there is little chance for the individual teacher to actually change the curriculum, but we can make the way we deliver the curriculum very different. And that's where the technology comes into play: to make it more interactive, to encourage collaborative learning, encourage exploration. The technology can adjust to fit the curriculum, I think, whatever it is.

Technology is not a panacea for educational reform, but it can be a significant catalyst for change. To those looking for a simple innovative solution, technology is not the answer. To those looking for a powerful tool to support collaborative learning environments, technology holds tremendous potential.

Methodological Appendix
References
About the Authors
Index

Methodological Appendix

The research reported in this book draws upon data collected over 10 years since the ACOT project began in 1985. This appendix provides additional information about data collection and analysis. The first section describes the research methodology used to examine teachers' experiences in the ACOT classrooms, and the second focuses on the research strategies used to investigate the creation, implementation, and impact of the ACOT Teacher Development Center project.

ACOT CLASSROOMS

Settings

Our qualitative study of ACOT classrooms used data from 32 elementary and secondary teachers in five schools located in four states. The ACOT sites represented a cross section of America's K–12 schools in terms of grade level, socioeconomic status, and community setting. Table 1.1 in Chapter 1 summarizes the characteristics of the original sites. Project teachers were all volunteers selected by individual school districts. Few had worked closely with technology before joining the project. Teachers ranged from novices with 1 or 2 years of experience to veterans with over 20 years in the classroom. They ranged in age from their mid-twenties to mid-fifties and represented various ethnic backgrounds. At the elementary sites most of the teachers were female, but at the high school site there were approximately the same number of male and female teachers in the project.

Each of these sites began with one classroom per school in the fall of 1986, with classrooms, staff, and students added in subsequent years. Although each site served students from a variety of grade levels, none of the sites encompassed an entire school. ACOT staff asked that the gender and ethnic composition of the classes mirror the school as a whole; all other decisions about student selection were left up to school personnel.

Students and teachers had constant access to interactive technologies in each of these settings. In the first year of the project ACOT equipped the high school with Macintosh computers and the elementary sites with Apple IIe, IIGS, and Macintosh computers. In addition to the computers, ACOT provided printers, scanners, laserdisc and videotape players, modems, CD-ROM drives, and a wide variety of software titles.

The technology was used as a tool to support learning across the curriculum. No attempt was made to replace existing instructional technologies with computers. Instead, the classrooms included—along with computers—multiple instructional resources such as textbooks, workbooks, manipulative math materials, whiteboards, crayons, paper, glue, overhead projectors, televisions, and pianos. The operating principle in ACOT classrooms was to use the media that best supported the learning goal.

Data Collection

The 32 ACOT teachers provided bimonthly audiotapes, on which they reflected about their experiences; weekly reports sent via electronic mail; and correspondence between sites. In addition, we reviewed reports of independent researchers who had observed in project classrooms to investigate the impact of technology on various aspects of learning and teaching.

Audiotape Journals.   Teachers recorded their personal observations of events in their classrooms and their reflections on those events on audiotape. Instructions about content on the tapes were purposefully left vague, leaving teachers free to report what was most salient at the time to each of them. These tapes were understood by the teachers to be research data that would be listened to and indexed by research staff. Teachers often took the opportunity to vent their frustrations and share their triumphs, giving the tapes an emotionally charged quality. Although the teachers differed with regard to how many tapes they made over the course of a year, each teacher produced, on average, two 60-minute tapes per month.

Weekly Reports.   The teaching staff at each site communicated weekly on major events and developments in written summaries that were electronically distributed to all project participants through Apple Computer's corporate networking system. Rather than asking teachers to comment on a particular aspect of their teaching, ACOT staff gave teachers freedom to report what was most salient to each of them at the time. Because these reports were publicly aired to everyone connected with the project, they tended to be more self-conscious than the personal, frequently introspective reports contained in the audiotape journals. Often they either provided corroboration of events mentioned in teachers' journals or revealed contrasts.

Correspondence Sent Between Sites (Site Links). Project teachers at each site communicated with teachers at other sites via Apple's electronic networking system. Teachers initiated this correspondence and typically solicited or offered information related to different software programs, equipment, or classroom activities.

Data Analysis

Unlike many researchers, who attempt to reduce qualitative data to quantifiable codes or symbols, we decided at the outset of this project to use as our data source the actual text information generated in the weekly reports, site links, and audiotapes. We wanted to develop an indexing system that would direct researchers to episodes illustrating specific content where the original textual data could be studied. We needed a system of data management that would remain flexible enough to allow us to investigate questions that evolved over time.

Researchers summarized the audiotapes and entered written communications verbatim into the database. To facilitate analysis, narratives were divided into episodes, each episode representing an event, with a beginning, middle, and end. Episodes were indexed for retrieval using a variety of categories and subcategories (for example, participant, affective tone, context, general theme). The development of content categories was an iterative process and followed the principles of "grounded theory" (Glaser & Strauss, 1967), "progressive focusing" (Hamilton, MacDonald, King, Jenkins, & Parlett, 1977) and "collapsing outlines" (Smith, 1978). Over the course of the project, the indexing system was revised and expanded numerous times. For example, during the second year of the project, it became clear that the thematic subcategories in the early coding system were too broad to be useful for detailed analysis, so we decided to further refine and define major categories and subcategories to ease data retrieval and analysis. The final indexing system allowed sorting and retrieval of descriptive, qualitative data along a number of dimensions for the construction of reports.

To assess the reliability of the indexing process, one of the researchers conducted a detailed analysis of inter-rater reliability (Keirns, 1990). She computed the inter-rater reliability for nine research indexers on three sample episodes, using a formula suggested by Miles & Huberman (1984, p. 63):

number of agreements / number of agreements + number of disagreements

The researcher analyzed the agreements among the staff in the selection of each index symbol in the 13 major categories indexed in the database. She computed agreement on the selection of an index as either present or not present and averaged agreements for each category. A total overall average of agreements for each episode was computed, yielding results of 89%, 91%, and 86% respectively. These reliability figures are within the range suggested as satisfactory by Miles and Huberman (1984) for groups of field workers dealing with similar data, and reflect the effect of considering pooled ratings described by Thorndike and Hagen (1986).

Over the years, the database expanded at a rapid rate and became unwieldy given the capacity of the technology at that time. We decided to divide it into two databases, which together had over 20,000 episodes. We used Double Helix, a relational database, to manage and analyze the data. This software program allows data to be organized in a multitude of ways. The database allowed us to organize a vast quantity of text data and retrieve them by individual variables such as grade level, school, individual, theme, and context, as well as combinations of these variables. Data from all project teachers were included in the analysis.

ACOT TEACHER DEVELOPMENT CENTER PROJECT

Settings

The ACOT teacher development centers opened in 1992 and are located in three of ACOT's oldest sites, including two elementary schools and one high school. At the centers, participating teachers observe and work with accomplished ACOT teachers and students during actual school days. Each teacher development center also has a coordinator. During the first year of the project, all participants who attended the centers came from the districts in which the centers are located. Site A is located in a district that has 18 elementary and 4 junior high schools. The district serves approximately 14,000 students, with a minority population of 35%. Site B is in a district of approximately 64,000 students, with a minority population of 52%. The district includes 92 schools and employs 4,650 teachers. Site C is located in a district serving 71,000 students in 121 schools. The minority population in the district is 43%. The ACOT program at this site includes a special education classroom.

In the project's second year, attendance was open to districts throughout the country. Over the course of three years, over 600 teachers from more than 30 districts participated in the project. Participants represented a variety of grade levels and disciplines, and included teachers in special education, Chapter 1, and bilingual education, as well as administrators, resource personnel, and librarians. Participants ranged from beginning teachers to veterans with over 30 years of experience. Teachers' technological knowledge and expertise ranged dramatically as well. Some had never used a computer before, but others rated their proficiency with technology as high. Chapter 9 describes the process of selecting participants for the centers as well as the program components.

Data Collection

In the ACOT Teacher Development Center project, the focus of our research varied over the course of the three years of data collection. During the first year, we focused on creating a rich description of program implementation at each site. In the second year, we investigated the impact of the program on participants. In the final year of the project, we continued studying program impact and also examined how the program was spreading through the schools. Specifically, we investigated the following questions:

- What qualities characterize a staff development program where teachers can acquire the skills they need to effectively integrate technology into their classrooms and utilize constructivist teaching techniques?
- What is the impact of the program on participating teachers' attitudes toward instruction, their role in the classroom, and their use of technology?
- What influence has the project had on participating teachers' schools and districts?
- What features of the school and district environment facilitate or hinder instructional and school change?

Data sources included pre- and post-interviews with participating teachers and ACOT teachers; pre-, post-, and follow-up questionnaires; a minimum of three formal interviews each year with program coordinators and informal interviews once a month; coordinators' weekly reports; participants' written journals; observations of each summer institute and a sample of practicums; and interviews with a random sample of principals who sent teachers to the program.

In the second year, we also conducted in-depth case studies of nine teachers (three from each site). These teachers represented a range of grade levels, teaching experience, and technological expertise. We further constrained the selection to ensure that the teachers' schools represented a range of contexts in terms of student socioeconomic status and amount of technology available.

Data collection for the case studies included periodic classroom observations; a minimum of three formal interviews with each teacher and follow-up interviews as needed; and audiotape journals in which they reflected on their use of technology, their ideas about teaching, and classroom and school events. Interviews with other teachers and administrators at the schools provided corroborating data about the case study teachers.

In the third year, we conducted case studies of six schools that had sent teachers to the centers. We viewed these schools as having the strongest potential to become second-generation teacher development centers. Data collection included interviews and observations of participating teachers, interviews with school administrators, and interviews of teachers who had not attended the teacher development centers.

Data Analysis

Data analysis focused extensively on determining the ways in which participation in the teacher development centers influenced the teachers and their schools. The pre- and post-interviews centered on teachers' beliefs about learning and instruction and on their expectations about the project. Pre-institute interviews focused on gathering baseline information regarding teachers' level of expertise and experience with various technological tools, alternative assessment strategies, team teaching, and collaborative/cooperative learning strategies. Observations and unstructured interviews during the institutes concentrated on assessing teachers' reactions to components of the program and documenting their concerns. Post-institute interviews focused on new levels of awareness stemming from participation in the centers, and documented teachers' project plans for the year, including how the plans would expand their own practices.

On-site coordinator reports, teacher self-report audiotape journals, weekly telecommunicated progress reports, and administrator interviews documented and corroborated the implementation and relative success of teachers' efforts. Questionnaires, observations, weekly reports, and interviews provided information about the types of follow-up support participants received and the barriers they faced upon returning to their schools. The use of in-depth case studies provided the opportunity to examine more closely changes in teachers' beliefs and instructional strategies that might not have been readily apparent with other research techniques.

To facilitate analysis, site researchers gathered relevant documents and took detailed field notes of observations and formal and informal interviews. Center coordinators submitted weekly reports and collected teachers' reflective journals. Researchers tape recorded and transcribed formal interviews and participated in regular debriefing sessions. Analysis of the qualitative data followed an iterative process typically employed in qualitative studies (Miles & Huberman, 1984). The process includes transcribing, coding, and annotating the data; creating data displays; seeking disconfirming and corroborative evidence; and identifying patterns, themes, and explanations. Where appropriate, basic descriptive statistical analysis was performed on questionnaire responses.

The multiple case study approach included within-case and cross-case analysis. Within-case analysis focused on developing an in-depth understanding of each individual case. Cross-case analysis provided comparisons across teachers and school contexts, and centered on exploring differences between participating teachers.

References

Ames, G., & Murray, F. B. (1982). When two wrongs make a right: Promoting cognitive change through social conflict. *Developmental Psychology, 18,* 894–897.

Applebee, A. N., Langer, J. A., & Mullis, I. (1989). *Crossroads in American education.* Princeton, NJ: Educational Testing Service.

Atherley, C. A. (1989). "Shared reading": An experiment in peer tutoring in the primary classroom. *Educational Studies, 15*(2), 145–153.

Baker, E. L., Herman, J. L., & Gearhart, M. (1989). *The ACOT report card: Effects on complex performance and attitude.* Paper presented at the meeting of the American Educational Research Association, San Francisco.

Baldridge, B. J., & Deal, T. E. (1975). *Managing change in educational organizations.* Berkeley, CA: McCutchan Publishing Corporation.

Barth, R. S. (1990). *Improving schools from within.* San Francisco: Jossey-Bass.

Becker, H. J. (1987, July). *The impact of computer use on children's learning: What research has shown and what it has not.* Baltimore, MD: Center for Research on Elementary and Middle Schools.

Berman, P., & McLaughlin, M. W. (1976). Implementation of educational innovation. *Educational Forum, 40*(3), 345–370.

Berry, B. (1995). School restructuring and teacher power: The case of Keels Elementary. In A. Lieberman (Ed.), *The work of restructuring schools: Building from the ground up.* New York: Teachers College Press.

Bork, A. (1991). The history of technology and education. In N. Knupfer, R. Muffoletto, M. McIsaac, A. Bork, R. Koetting, & A. Yeaman (Eds.), *Educational computing social foundations: A symposium.* (ERIC Document Reproduction Service No. ED 334 990).

Bowers, D. G. (1973). OD techniques and their results in 23 organizations: The Michigan ICL study. *Journal of Applied Behavioral Science, 9,* 21–41.

Boyer, E. (1984). *Report of a panel on preparation of beginning teachers.* The Carnegie Foundation for the Advancement of Teaching. Princeton, NJ: Henry Chauncey Center.

Bracey, G. W. (1991). Why can't they be like we were? *Phi Delta Kappan, 73*(2), 104–118.

Bright, G. (1988). Time-on-task in computer and non-computer estimation games. *Journal of Computers in Mathematics and Science Teaching, 7*(4), 41–46.

Brooks J. G., & Brooks, M. G. (1993). *In search of understanding: The case for constructivist classrooms.* Alexandria, VA: Association for Supervision and Curriculum Development.

Brophy, J. (1988). Educating teachers about managing classrooms and students. *Teaching and Teacher Education, 4*(1), 1018.

Buber, M. (1957). *Between man and man.* Boston: Beacon Press.

Butt, R. L. (1984). *Curriculum implementation, classroom change and professional development: The challenge for supervision.* Paper presented at the annual meeting of the Canadian Society for the Study of Education, Ontario, Canada.

California Department of Education. (1992). *It's Elementary! Elementary Grades Task Force Report.* Sacramento, CA: California Department of Education.

Carnegie Forum on Education and the Economy. (1986). *A nation prepared: Teachers for the twenty-first century.* New York: Carnegie Corporation of New York.

Charters, W. (1980). *Formal organization and faculty communication: A study of the multiunit elementary school.* Eugene, OR: Center for Educational Policy and Management.

Chesterfield, R. A., & Chesterfield, K. B. (1985). "Hoja's with the H": Spontaneous peer teaching in bilingual classrooms. *Bilingual Review, 12*(3), 198–208.

Chin, R., & Benne, K. D. (1961). General strategies for effecting changes in human systems. In W. G. Bennis, K. D. Benne, & R. Chin (Eds.), *The planning of change.* New York: Holt, Rinehart & Winston.

Collins, A. (1991). The role of computer technology in restructuring schools. *Phi Delta Kappan, 73*(1), 28–36.

Common, D. (1983). Who should have the power to change schools: Teachers or policy makers? *Education-Canada, 23*(2), 40–45.

Corcoran, T. B. (1988). *Schoolwork: Perspectives on workplace reform in the public schools* (CRC 88-600). Stanford, CA: Center for Research on the Context of Secondary School Teaching.

Costello, R. (1987). Improving student achievement by overcoming teacher isolation. *The Clearing House, 61*(2), 91–93.

Cotton, K. (1982). Effects of interdisciplinary team teaching. *Research synthesis.* Portland, OR: Northwest Regional Educational Lab.

Cuban, L. (1984). *How teachers taught: Constancy and change in American classrooms 1890–1980.* New York: Longman.

Cuban, L. (1986). *Teachers and machines: The classroom use of technology since 1920.* New York: Teachers College Press.

Cuban, L. (1990). Reforming again, again, and again. *Educational Researcher, 19*(19), 3–13.

Cuban, L. (1991, September 29). The secret about U.S. test scores. *San Jose Mercury News,* pp. C1, C5.

Damarin, S., & Bohren, J. (1987). The evolution of the ACOT-Columbus classroom. In S. Damarin, & J. Bohren (Eds.), *Reaching for tomorrow: A study of a computer-saturated classroom.* Unpublished manuscript.

Darling-Hammond, L. (1990). Achieving our goals: Superficial or structural reforms. *Phi Delta Kappan, 19*(19), 286–295.

Dedicott, W. (1986). Paired storying. *Reading, 20*(3), 168–172.

Dewey, J. (1963). *Experience and education.* New York: Collier Books.

Doyle, W. (1980). *Classroom management.* West Lafayette, IN: Kappa Delta Phi.

Doyle, W. (1986). Classroom organization and management. In M. C. Wittrock (Ed.), *Handbook of research on teaching* (3rd ed., pp. 392–431). New York: Macmillan.

Dwyer, D. (1981). *Ideology and organizational evolution: A comparative study of two innovative educational projects.* Unpublished doctoral dissertation, Washington University, St. Louis, MO.

Dwyer, D. (1994). Apple Classrooms of Tomorrow: What we've learned. *Educational Leadership, 51*(7), 4–10.

Dwyer, D., Ringstaff, C., & Sandholtz, J. H. (1991). Changes in teachers' beliefs and practices in technology-rich classrooms. *Educational Leadership, 48*(8).

Educational Technology Center. (1985). *Teacher as learner: The impact of technology.* Cambridge, MA.

Fish, M., & Feldman, S. (1988). Teacher and student verbal behavior in microcomputer classes: An observational study. *Journal of Classroom Interaction, 23*(1), 15–21.

Fisher, C. W. (1991). Some influences of classroom computers on academic tasks. *Journal of Computing in Childhood Education, 2*(2), 3–16.

Fosnot, C. T. (1989). *Enquiring teachers, enquiring learners: A constructivist approach for teaching.* New York: Teachers College Press.

Fosnot, C. T. (1992) Constructing constructivism. In T. M. Duffy, & D. H. Jonassen (Eds.), *Constructivism and the technology of instruction: A conversation.* New Jersey: Lawrence Erlbaum Associates.

Fullan, M. G. (1982). *The meaning of educational change.* New York: Teachers College Press.

Fullan, M. G. (1990). Staff development, innovation, and institutional development. In B. Joyce, (Ed.). *1990 Yearbook of the Association for Supervision and Curriculum Development.* Alexandria, VA: Association for Supervision and Curriculum Development.

Fullan, M. G., & Stiegelbauer, S. (1991). *The new meaning of educational change.* New York: Teachers College Press.

Gearhart, M., Herman, J., Baker, E., & Novak, J. (1990). *A new mirror for the classroom: The effects of technology in instruction.* Paper presented at the annual meeting of the American Educational Research Association, Boston.

Gersten, R., & Guskey, T. (1985). *Transforming teacher reluctance to teacher commitment.* Paper presented at the annual meeting of the American Educational Research Association, Chicago.

Giacquinta, J. B. (1973). The process of organizational change in schools. In F. N. Kerlinger (Ed.), *Review of Research in Education, 3* (pp. 178–208). Itasca, IL: Peacock.

Glaser, B., & Strauss, A. (1967). *The discovery of grounded theory.* Chicago: Aldine Publishing.

Greene, M. (1979). Teaching: the question of personal reality. In A. Lieberman & L. Miller (Eds.), *Staff development: New demands, new realities, new perspectives* (pp. 23–35). New York: Teachers College, Columbia University.

Gross, N., & Herriott, R. E. (Eds.). (1979). *The dynamics of planned educational change.* Berkeley, CA: McCutchan Publishing Corporation.

Hamilton, D., MacDonald, B., King, C., Jenkins, D., & Parlett, M. (1977). *Beyond the numbers game.* London: MacMillan Education Ltd.

Hargreaves, A. (1994). *Changing teachers, changing times.* London: Cassell.

Hawkins J., Sheingold K., Gearhart, M., & Berger, C. (1982). Microcomputers in schools: Impact on the social life of elementary classrooms. *Journal of Applied Developmental Psychology, 3,* 361–373.

Henson, K. (1987). Strategies for overcoming barriers to educational change. *NASSP Bulletin, 71*(497), 125–127.

Hiebert, E. H., Quellmalz, E. S., & Vogel, P. (1989). *A research based writing program for students with high access to computers* (ACOT Report No. 2). Cupertino, CA: Apple Computer.

Hoffer, E. (1951). *The true believer: Thoughts on the nature of mass movements.* New York: Perennial Library Harper & Row.

Holmes Group. (1990). *Tomorrow's schools: Principles for the design of professional development schools.* East Lansing, MI: The Holmes Group.

Janis, I. (1972). *The victims of group think: A psychological study of foreign-policy decisions and fiascoes.* Boston: Houghton-Mifflin.

Johnston, J., & Joscelyn, M. (1989). *The computer revolution in teaching.* National Center for Research to Improve Secondary Teaching and Learning, Office of Educational Research and Improvement.

Jones, V. (1996). Classroom management. In J. Sikula (Ed.), *Handbook of research on teacher education* (2nd ed., pp. 503–521). New York: Macmillan.

Joyce, B. (1982). Organizational homeostasis and innovation: Tightening the loose couplings. *Education and Urban Society, 15*(1), 42–69.

Kelley, L. (1994). *Teachers at the center of educational reform: Professional development and the culture of schools as facilitators of change.* Unpublished manuscript.

Keirns, J. (1990). *Effects of immediate computer access on teachers' beliefs and practices: A longitudinal case study of the reflections of three teachers.* Unpublished doctoral dissertation, University of Southern California, Los Angeles, CA.

Knupfer, N. (1991). Educational computing and teachers: Changing roles, changing pedagogy. In N. Knupfer, R. Muffoletto, M. McIsaac, A. Bork, R. Koetting, & A. Yeaman (Eds.), *Educational computing social foundations: A symposium.* (ERIC Document Reproduction Service No. ED 334 990).

Land, W. A. (1984). *Peer tutoring: Student achievement and self-concept as reviewed in selected literature.* Paper presented at the annual conference of the Mid-South Educational Research Association, New Orleans, LA.

Latham, G., & Stoddard, C. (1986). *Time on task analysis of the Logan High School Wandah project*. Unpublished report, Wasatch Institute for Research and Evaluation, Logan, UT.

Lewis, A. C. (1994). Developing good staff development. *Phi Delta Kappan*, 75(7), 508–509.

Lieberman, A. (1995). Restructuring schools: The dynamics of changing practice, structure, and culture. In A. Lieberman (Ed.), *The work of restructuring schools: Building from the ground up*. New York: Teachers College Press.

Lieberman, A., Saxl, E. R., & Miles, M. B. (1988). Teacher leadership: Ideology and practice. In A. Lieberman (Ed.), *Building a professional culture in schools*. New York: Teachers College Press.

Little, J. (1982). Norms of collegiality and experimentation: Workplace conditions of school success. *American Educational Research Journal*, 84(4), 493–511.

Lortie, D. C. (1975). *Schoolteacher*. Chicago: University of Chicago Press.

MacArthur, C., Haynes, J., & Malouf, D. (1986). Learning disabled students' engaged time and classroom interaction: The impact of computer assisted instruction. *Journal of Educational Computing Research*, 2(2), 189–197.

Magliaro, S., & Borko, H. (1986). A naturalistic investigation of experienced teachers' and student teachers' instructional practices. *Teaching and Teacher Education*, 2(2), 127–137.

Maheady, L., & Sainato, D. M. (1985). The effects of peer tutoring upon the social status and social interaction patterns of high and low status elementary school students. *Education and Treatment of Children*, 8(1), 51–65.

McCaslin, M., & Good, T. (1992). Compliant cognition: The misalliance of management and instructional goals in current school reform. *Educational Researcher*, 21(3), 4–17.

McGarity, J., & Butts, D. (1984). The relationship among teacher classroom management behavior, student engagement, and student achievement of middle and high school science students of varying aptitude. *Journal of Research in Science Teaching*, 21(1), 55–61.

Means, B. (1994). Introduction: Using technology to advance instructional goals. In B. Means (Ed.), *Technology and education reform: The reality behind the promise*. San Francisco: Jossey-Bass.

Mehlinger, H. D. (1996). School reform in the information age. *Phi Delta Kappan*, 77(6), 400–407.

Memphis Public Schools. (1987). ACOT: Right here in Memphis. *Memphis District Newsletter*, Memphis, TN.

Metz, M. H. (1988). Some missing elements in the educational reform movement. *Educational Administration Quarterly*, 24(4), 446–460.

Mevarech, Z. (1986). Time engagement and achievement in CAI. *Educational Technology*, 26(7), 38–40.

Miles, M., & Huberman, A. (1984). *Qualitative data analysis*. Thousand Oaks, CA: Sage.

Miller, L. (1988). Unlikely beginnings: The district office as a starting point for developing a professional culture for teaching. In A. Lieberman (Ed.), *Building a professional culture in schools*. New York: Teachers College Press.

Miller, L., & Olson, J. (1995). How computers live in schools. *Educational Leadership, 53*(2), 74–77.

Nespor, J. (1987). The role of beliefs in the practice of teaching. *Journal of Curriculum Studies, 19*(4), 317–328.

Noddings, N. (1990). Constructivism in mathematics education. In R. Davis, C. Maher, & N. Noddings (Eds.), *Constructivist views on the teaching and learning of mathematics*. Reston, VA: National Council of Teachers of Mathematics.

Office of Technology Assessment. (1988). *Power on! New tools for teaching and learning*. Washington, DC: U.S. Government Printing Office.

Office of Technology Assessment. (April 1995). *Teachers and technology: Making the connection* (OTA-CHR-616). Washington, DC: U.S. Government Printing Office.

Papert, S. (1980). *Mindstorms: Children, computers, and powerful ideas*. New York: Basic Books.

Paul, D. A. (1977). Change processes at the elementary, secondary and post secondary levels of education. In N. Nash & J. Culbertson (Eds.), *Linking processes in educational improvement: Concepts and applications* (pp. 7–73). Columbus, OH: University Council for Educational Administration.

Pepi, D., & Scheurman, G. (1996). The emperor's new computer: A critical look at our appetite for computer technology. *Journal of Teacher Education, 47*(3), 229–236.

Perkins, V. (1988). Effective instruction using microcomputers. *Academic Therapy, 24*(2), 129–135.

Phelan, P. (1989). *The addition of computers to a first-grade classroom: A case study of two children*. Unpublished report.

Phelps, E., & Damon, W. (1989). Problem solving with equals: Peer collaboration as a context for learning mathematics and spatial concepts. *Journal of Educational Psychology, 81*(4), 639–646.

Purkey, S. C., & Smith, M. S. (1983). Effective schools—a review. *Elementary School Journal, 83*, 427–452.

Reed, S. (1990). The write team: Getting a foot in the door. *English Journal, 79*(3), 67–69.

Rokeach, M. (1975). *Beliefs, attitudes and values*. San Francisco: Jossey-Bass.

Rutherford, W. (1981). *Team teaching—How do teachers use it?* Austin, TX: Research and Development Center for Teacher Education.

Rutter, M., Maughan, B., Mortimore, P., & Ouston, J. (1979). *Fifteen thousand hours: Secondary schools and their effects on children*. Cambridge, MA: Harvard University Press.

Sandholtz, J. H. (1989). *The department as context for secondary school teaching*. Unpublished doctoral dissertation, Stanford University, Stanford, CA.

Schein, E. H. (1985). *Organizational culture and leadership: A dynamic view* (1st ed.). San Francisco: Jossey-Bass.

Schiffer, J. (1979). A framework for staff development. In A. Lieberman & L. Miller (Eds.), *Staff development: New demands, new realities, new perspectives* (pp. 4–23). New York: Teachers College Press.

Schmidt, D., & Kane, J. (1984). Solving an identity crisis. *Principal, 63*(3), 32–35.

Secretary's Commission on Achieving Necessary Skills (SCANS). (July, 1991). *What work requires of schools: A SCANS Report for America 2000.* Washington, DC: U.S. Department of Labor.

Sheingold, K. (1991). Restructuring for learning with technology: The potential for synergy. *Phi Delta Kappan 73*(1), 17–27.

Sigurdson, S. (1982). *Two years on the block plan: Meeting the needs of junior high school students.* Edmonton, Alberta, Canada: Alberta Department of Education.

Sikula, J. (1996). *Handbook of research on teacher education* (2nd ed.). New York: Macmillan.

Sizer, T. R. (1984). *Horace's compromise: The dilemma of the American high school.* Boston: Houghton-Mifflin.

Slavin, R. E. (1983). *Cooperative learning.* New York: Longman.

Smith, B. O. (1963). Toward a theory of teaching. In A. A. Bellack (Ed.), *Theory and research in teaching.* New York: Bureau of Publications, Teachers College.

Smith, L. M. (1978). An evolving logic of participant observation, educational ethnography and other case studies. In L. Shulman (Ed.), *Review of research in education.* Itaska, IL: Peacock.

Smith, L. M., & Dwyer, D. C. (1979). *Federal policy in action: A case study of an urban education project.* Washington DC: Occasional Paper of the National Institute of Education.

Smylie, M., & Tuermer, U. (1995). Restructuring schools in Hammond, Indiana. In A. Lieberman (Ed.), *The work of restructuring schools: Building from the ground up.* New York: Teachers College Press.

Swanson-Owens, D. (1985). *Identifying natural sources of resistance: A case study analysis of curriculum implementation.* Paper presented at the annual meeting of the American Education Research Association, Chicago.

Thorndike, R., & Hagen, E. (1986). *Measurement and evaluation in psychology and education* (4th ed.). New York: Macmillan.

Tierney, R. J., Kieffer, R. D., Whalin, K., Desai, L., & Gale, A. (1992). *A longitudinal study of the influence of high computer access on students' thinking, learning, and interactions* (ACOT Report No. 16). Cupertino, CA: Apple Computer.

Veenman, S. (1984). Perceived problems of beginning teachers. *Review of Educational Research, 54*(2), 143–178.

Wang, M., Haertel, G., & Walberg, H. (1993). Toward a knowledge base for school learning. *Review of Educational Research, 63*(3), 249–294.

Whitford, B., & Gaus, D. M. (1995) With a little help from their friends: Teachers making change at Wheeler School. In A. Lieberman (Ed.), *The work of restructuring schools: Building from the ground up.* New York: Teachers College Press.

Willis, J., & Mehlinger, H. (1996). Information technology and teacher education. In J. Sikula (Ed.), *Handbook of research on teacher education* (2nd ed., pp. 978–1029). New York: Macmillan.

Wilson, R. (1987). Direct observation of academic learning time. *Teaching Exceptional Children, 19*(2), 13–17.

Zuk, D., & Danner, F. (1986). *The effects of microcomputers on children's attention to reading tasks.* Paper presented at the annual meeting of the American Educational Research Association, San Francisco.

About the Authors

Judith Haymore Sandholtz is Director of the Comprehensive Teacher Education Institute at the University of California, Riverside. She holds a Ph.D. in education and an Ed.S. in program evaluation from Stanford University. Her teaching experience ranges from a private elementary school in South America to a public high school in the United States to the university level. Her research and writing focus on teacher development, school/university partnerships, professional development schools, and technology-rich classrooms.

Cathy Ringstaff, a former teacher, completed her Ph.D. in Educational Psychology and her Ed.S. in evaluation at Stanford University, with a special emphasis on the evaluation of educational programs and research on teaching. As an independent research consultant, Dr. Ringstaff has worked with numerous school districts, universities, and private education foundations as a specialist in evaluation. She has also conducted a variety of studies for Apple Computer, SRI International, and the National Center for Education and the Economy, investigating the impact of technology on teaching and learning.

David C. Dwyer is Vice President for Advanced Learning Technologies at Computer Curriculum Corporation in Sunnyvale, California. He began his education career as a secondary science teacher and was twice recognized as an Outstanding Secondary Educator of America. He earned a Ph.D. in educational innovation and policy from Washington University in 1981 and has focused his work on educational leadership, innovation, and change in American schools, and technology in education. As an Apple Distinguished Scientist, Dr. Dwyer directed the research and development efforts of Apple Classrooms of Tomorrow (ACOT) and was program manager for most of ACOT's first decade.

Index